EDGWARE ROAD

FROM ROMANS TO ROMANIANS AND EVERYONE IN BETWEEN

EDGWARE ROAD

FROM ROMANS TO ROMANIANS AND EVERYONE IN BETWEEN

LÉO WOODLAND

The History Press

First published 2024

The History Press
97 St George's Place, Cheltenham,
Gloucestershire, GL50 3QB
www.thehistorypress.co.uk

British Library Cataloguing in Publication Data.
A catalogue record for this book is available from the British Library.

ISBN 978 1 80399 627 1

Typesetting and origination by The History Press
Printed and bound in Great Britain by TJ Books Limited, Padstow, Cornwall.

Trees for Life

CONTENTS

Has there ever been a road so short yet so colourful? Well, maybe. A lot has happened in the world, after all. But history has been made on this road, nevertheless, and not always happily. The mere 10 miles of the Edgware Road as it leans lazily northwards out of London take some beating when it comes to social history in Britain. They and its surrounding streets have seen advancing invaders, public executions, highwaymen, an insurrection, murderers and gangsters, a Great Train Robber and a naturist 'riot'. And the birth of Tesco, and a workhouse so cruel that those who lived nearby preferred to call their town something else. Plus the roots of modern aviation.

Every nation on earth has settled along the road. Arab immigrants and their successors post signs in gorgeous curling writing outside their shops. The Irish came here, too, to build roads and houses, to find themselves exploited and ruined, to fight in the street and, as a sad song puts it, 'to work 'til they're dead for a room and a bed'. The Jewish population grew so large that it has the nation's largest synagogue. Mosques dot the length of the highway. Sikhs built a gurdwara at Brent and Hindus their temples.

There are Romanians in Burnt Oak, a south Indian population in Edgware, and the road has an inter-war housing estate for rehoused slum dwellers that was of such leafy design that Burnt Oak station for many years pointed out that it was 'for Watling'.

Will you join me for a walk through time and history?

1777

LADY HAMILTON'S SCANDALS

She was as beautiful as a butterfly and as proud as a queen, was Pretty Polly Perkins of Paddington Green.

Where's that from? From a song from Victorian times. Harry Clifton wrote and sang it as he toured the music halls. It's about a milkman who falls in love with the maid he sees in a gentleman's house as he goes about his round. He asks her to marry him. 'What stuff!' she scoffs, and she sends him on his way, broken-hearted.

Paddington Green is at the south of Edgware Road. It was quite the area in Polly Perkins' day, enough so that those who lived there could employ butlers, cooks and maids. It still had the air of the villages of Paddington and Lilestone that formed it. It's rather less salubrious now; when the BBC filmed a series there in late 1998, its characters included a transexual prostitute, a jack-the-lad in the car park business, and a teenage model. A series 200 years earlier would have included Emma Hamilton. She too lived in Paddington Green. And she was Nelson's lover, of course.

Emma was conniving, flirtatious and quick to profit from any situation at someone else's expense. She changed her name when it suited her. She frequented high society but the Prince of Wales was sure he'd seen her working as a prostitute in Covent Garden. Her names included Emma Lyon, Hart, Hartley and Hamilton. It makes her hard to follow.

What we know is that she was born into poverty in Cheshire in 1765. She was known then as Emy Lyon. Sometime around her 12th birthday she made her way to London. She became a maid for a Dr Budd of Bart's Hospital, at his home south of the Thames in Chatham Place, Blackfriars. She worked there with another youngster, Jane Powell, who dreamed of becoming an actress. Both girls agreed it was better than working as a skivvy. And maybe they dreamed enough that they didn't get on with their work, because Budd sacked both within a year.

They crossed the Thames to mingle in what another era called the *demi-monde* of Covent Garden. Powell did become an actress but Emy ended up behind the scenes in the costume department of Thomas Linley's Theatre Royal, in Drury Lane. She earned extra cash by dancing as a classical goddess at so-called sex therapy courses run by James Graham at his Temple of Health in the Strand. He claimed to have invented or discovered electrical aether and nervous aetherial balsam. Girls dressed, or more probably dressed lightly, as classical goddesses helped gentlemen with their recovery.

That may strike us as faintly shocking now but it was less so then. Many women worked as prostitutes, and not always the lowly. Emy will have seen prostitutes in Covent Garden and she was once identified as one there. Most were in their 20s and, like Emy, from outside London. Prostitution was common and open, so common that nobody knew how many prostitutes there were. A magistrate, Patrick Colquhoun, reckoned 50,000. Others were more cautious and said 6,000 or 7,000.

The most prolific of the 'scarlet ladies' was Charlotte Hayes, often referred to as Madame Kelly. She was Irish, as her name suggests, but not at all restricted to Ireland. Her ventures included an upmarket brothel, Le Chabanais, near the Louvre. And forget grubby workmen with a bottle of absinthe in one hand and half a baguette in the other: her customers included the future Edward VII, the artist Toulouse-Lautrec and, long afterwards, Humphrey Bogart and Cary Grant.

Madame Kelly also opened a brothel in Soho, expanded to St James's and then elsewhere. Emy joined her as a servant. She was 14. There is no sign that she joined the troupe of *horizontales* but there's little reason to suppose she didn't. In any case, it was that there she met Sir Harry Fetherstonhaugh, a 'witless playboy' according to those who knew him and a man who, as MP for Portsmouth, never once spoke in the House of Commons. He invited her – some say bought her – to join him at his country estate at Uppark House, a majestic building of two floors and an attic near Petersfield in West Sussex. She lived there in a cottage, from which she emerged to entertain friends by, it's said, dancing naked on a table.

Fetherstonhaugh threw her out when she became pregnant. His friend, Charles Greville, another Member of Parliament, took her in once she'd agreed to give away her daughter, also called Emma, to change her name, and to never see Fetherstonhaugh again.

Emy, now calling herself Emma Hart, moved into Greville's house in Paddington Green in 1782. There, he passed her on to his uncle, William Hamilton, the British ambassador in Naples. Emma joined him in Italy on her 21st birthday, 26 April 1786. They married five years later in the old Marylebone parish church at the top of Marylebone Lane – it's now a sandwich shop – before returning to Naples, where she became a society wow. She married under her original name of Emma Lyon.

It was in Naples that she met the admiral, Horatio Nelson. He wanted a mistress and Emma wanted a celebrity date. They began a *ménage à trois* at 23 Piccadilly with the elderly Lord Hamilton. She had Nelson's daughter there, Horatia, and the gossip became overwhelming. They fled central London. Nelson paid £9,000 for Merton Place in 1801 and called it Paradise Merton. It stood in Merton High Street in what is now south-west London. The ground floor was cramped but upstairs were eight bedrooms.

Hamilton died in 1803. He left Emma a small pension but the estate went to Charles Greville. Nelson died at Trafalgar two years later. Once again, Emma didn't get a lot out of her loss. His brother got all the land and houses except Merton, and Emma received the house, £500 a year and £2,000 in cash. It was a fortune then, it's true, but far less than she'd been used to and not enough to maintain Paradise Merton. Her money dwindled to the point at which she turned to friends to help her sell the house and to carry on living there at a nominal rent. The lavish life had gone, though, and she took to the bottle. Her creditors caught up with her, and in 1813 she went to a debtors' prison.

That could have been worse; the rules for 'genteel' prisoners allowed them to spend their sentence not in a cell but at a house near the jail. Even that was more than she could tolerate and she determined to flee abroad. On 1 July 1814, she boarded a private boat and sailed to Calais with £50 in her purse. There, she lived at the Hôtel Dessin, described as the best in town. She continued spending on credit, living with a housekeeper and servants. Her health worsened and so did her credit. Religion seemed the only answer and she turned to the Roman Catholic Church.

Then the money ran out for good. She and Horatia moved into a single room at 27 rue Française in the port area. The district has been rebuilt after wartime bombing and her flat no longer exists, the nearest being a modern beauty parlour at No. 23. By then she was addicted to laudanum, a mixture of opium and alcohol. She died on 15 January 1815, aged just 49, and she was buried beside the church in the rue du Four. The upright stone, green with age, referred to her as Emma Lady Hamilton. It recorded her name, dates of birth and death, and that she was married to William Hamilton. Emma's date of birth was first written as 15 Jannary; rather than start anew, the stonemason added a loop below the legs of the second N. The grave was destroyed in the war, but a memorial to her has stood since 1994 in the nearby Parc Richelieu.

She had fallen a long way, had Pretty Polly Perkins of Paddington Green.

1810

CURRY COMES TO LONDON

Chicken tikka masala, said a foreign secretary, is Britain's national dish. Traditionalists demanded Robin Cook's head for such treason. But even they couldn't deny that, first, curry had made great inroads into British culture and that, second, chicken tikka masala is so British that it's unknown in India and Pakistan. The masala sauce that gives its distinctive taste was added only to suit British tastes.

There are so-called Indian restaurants – in fact more often owned by Pakistanis with Bengali chefs – on almost every town's high street. Their roots are in the East India Company, a private venture given the right to develop trade with India but which in the end both conquered and administered it. It had a private army larger than the Queen's. Only when the company failed, despite being able to rob the great wealth that once existed in India, did the government take over India's administration itself.

By then, countless employees and civil servants had developed a taste for the food they found there, and they brought that longing home with them. Norris Street Coffee House served curry in the Haymarket, London, as early as 1733. More restaurants grew up around Piccadilly in the next fifty years. But not until 1810 did a purely curry restaurant open, run by an Indian. It was then that the Hindoostane Coffee House opened just off the Edgware Road at 34, now 102, George Street. It's between Gloucester Place and Baker Street. The owner was Dean Mahomed, a Bengali traveller, surgeon, entrepreneur and a captain in the East India Company.

Mahomed, sometimes spelled Muhammad, was born in Bihari in Bengal, the northeast of the country, in 1759. He joined the East India Company's private army when he was 11. He rose to become a captain, stayed with the army until 1782 and then emigrated to Cork, in Ireland. There he married a local girl, Jane Daly, the daughter of a wealthy family. She was a 'fair and beautiful' fellow student 'of a family of rank'. Her portrait shows her as square-faced with wide-spaced eyes, a prominent nose and a small mouth. She would not now be considered a beauty.

Some accounts say that Mahomed married again, bigamously because Jane was still alive. The second wife is also said to have been called Jane. Much about Mahomed's life is unclear or simply invention but it seems probable that there was just the one Jane, that the couple eloped and lived together, their marriage delayed by being of different religions. That would account for claims of bigamy. In any case, Jane's name appears as his wife on his gravestone.

Jane and Mahomed moved to Portman Square when he was about 50 – remember that little is clear – and there they joined other former employees of the East India Company. He guessed that they'd like a taste from their past and he opened the Hindoostane Dinner and Hooka Smoking Club in 1810. The name shortened to the Hindoostane Coffee House.

The *Morning Post* announced on 2 February 1810:

Sake Dean Mahomed, manufacturer of the real currie powder, takes the earliest opportunity to inform the nobility and gentry, that he has, under the patron- age of the first men of quality who have resided in India, established at his house, 34 George Street, Portman Square, the Hindoostane Dinner and Hooka Smoking Club. Apartments are fitted up for their entertainment in the Eastern style, where dinners, composed of genuine Hindoostane dishes, are served up at the shortest notice ... Such ladies and gentlemen as may desirous of having India Dinners dressed and sent to their own houses will be punctually attended to by giving previous notice.

The *Times* advertised on 27 March 1811:

Mahomed, East-Indian, informs the Nobility and Gentry, he has fitted up the above house, neatly and elegantly, for the entertainment of Indian gentlemen, where they may enjoy the Hoakha, with real Chilm tobacco [from a village in Pakistan], and Indian dishes, in the highest perfection, and allowed by the greatest epicures to be unequalled to any curries ever made in England with choice wines.

Mahomed miscalculated, however. His neighbours did indeed like curry but they had their own cooks at home to prepare it. They saw no reason to go out to eat other peo- ple's food or to ask for it to be brought to their door. Mahomed belatedly realised his mistake. His money was running out. He sold his restaurant within a year and he became bankrupt. He then opened a spa in Brighton, at 102 King's Road where the Queen's Hotel now stands, and offered shampoos with Indian oils. A sign in capitals, the width of the building, announced 'Mahomed's Baths'. Legend says, or maybe he himself said, that he was the so-called shampooing surgeon to King George IV and William IV.

He advertised himself as the 'inventor of the Indian Medicated Vapour Baths', adding a decade to his age to make himself sound more convincing. 'What six or seven hours rest will produce in cases of fatigue, the vapour baths and shampooing will effect in a few minutes,' he wrote. 'The herbs of which my bath are impregnated are brought expressly from India and undergo a certain process known only to myself.' Customers relaxed in a bath infused with Indian oils and herbs until they perspired. They were then put into a cloth tent through which a masseur could rub them vigorously. Or if the customer was a woman, through which Jane could do the massaging. Clifford Musgrave's work *Life in Brighton* (1970) says:

> The fashionable invalids were eager for some fresh way of whiling away their time, and the highly scented steam baths were found by many to be far more agreeable than sea-water baths, whether hot or cold, and to sufferers from rheumatism and kindred ailments the massage was soothing and relaxing. There was, moreover, the intriguing sensation that one was enjoying something of the voluptuous indulgences of the East.

The process may not have been entirely pleasant, however. An unconvinced writer likened it to 'stewing alive by steam, sweetened by being forced through odoriferous herbs … dabbed all the while with pads of flannel'.

Mahomed persisted in his self-appointed title of 'Sake', the 'venerable one'. His shampoos, he insisted, were 'a cure to many diseases and giving full relief when everything fails; particularly rheumatic and paralytic, gout, stiff joints, old sprains, lame legs, aches and pains in the joints'. He hung certificates and testimonials on the walls of the building's plush entrance, along with crutches that he claimed customers had abandoned, Lourdes-style, thanks to his miracle oils. One letter read: 'I am very unwilling to leave your house without acknowledging my gratitude for the wonderful cure effected on Mrs Wartnaby by the use of your Vapour baths and advice.' Another enthused: 'Through the divine blessing, you have been the means of so much benefit to my bodily health, that I cannot leave this place without testifying my gratitude to you upon that account.'

Mahomed could blunder in his quest for publicity, however. The testimonials were not always spontaneous. One begins: 'In compliance with your request of yesterday's date, I feel much pleasure in stating, for the benefit of whomsoever it may concern, that, in the year 1816, I was completely crippled from contractions in both legs, and that from the use of your bath for six weeks, I found myself greatly recovered.'

It got Mohamed nowhere. Vapour baths soon became commonplace, cheaper, and better known as Turkish baths. Shampoo, once unknown, was no longer novel. He complained:

Several pretenders have, since my establishment has formed, entered the field in opposition to me who profess to know the art. Yet I am sure their ignorance must appear manifest to the world. It is a pity the public should be deluded by mere pretenders who bring into disrepute by their bungling stupidity the legitimate practice of a most useful and beneficial discovery.

Mohamed moved into a modest house in Black Lion Street and died at his son's home at 32 Grand Parade in December 1850, the year his vapour baths were demolished. He claimed to be 101 years old. His plaque in St Nicholas' churchyard reads:

Sacred to the memory of SAKE DEEN MAHOMED of PATNA HINDOOSTAN who died on the 25th of February 1851 aged 101 years and JANE his wife who died on the 26th of December 1850 aged 70 years. Sacred to the memory of ROSANNA, daughter of SAKE DEEN MAHOMED of PATNA HINDOOSTAN and JANE his wife, who departed this life January 7th 1818 aged 3 years also of HENRY EDWIN MAHOMED their son who departed this life January 30th 1823 aged 12 years.

There's a circular blue plaque on the Queen's Hotel to mark the site of his venture. It was paid for by the Chattri Memorial Group, which maintains a memorial to the Indian dead of the First World War on the Downs near Patcham. It was there that Hindus and Sikhs who died in Brighton's war hospitals were cremated. The Prince of Wales unveiled it on 21 February 1921. A green plaque put up in London by Westminster Council records the 'site of Hindoostane coffee house 1810, London's first Indian restaurant. Owned by Sake Dean Mahomed 1759–1851.'

It wasn't the end of curry, of course. Mahomed was simply ahead of his time. Progress, however, was slow. The *Independent*, covering the life of Sake Dean Mahomed, reported that there were just six Indian restaurants in Britain before the Second World War. But, says the same report, Indians who came to rebuild London after the Blitz went on to open cafés and canteens for their own communities. From there they opened restaurants for the established population, sometimes in bombed-out fish-and-chip shops. There, they sold curry and rice alongside more traditional food. Fish and chips and other meals vanished as customers developed a taste for Indian dishes. Seeking a formula, restaurants copied each other in putting waiters in dinner jackets and pasting red flock paper on the walls.

And chicken tikka masala, invented in Britain and sold only to Britons, became the national dish. According to one politician, anyway.

1820

DEATH TO THE RULING CLASS

Guy Fawkes and chums weren't the last to have a down on politicians. Walk for six streets along the Edgware Road from the Marble Arch and then turn right into Harrowby Street in front of the Argos shop. Pass one junction to the left, which is Brendon Street, and walk on to a covered alleyway also to the left, between a dry cleaner's and a barber's shop. It leads to Cato Street. No. 1a in Cato Street looks like a modernised stable, which indeed it is. Between its upper windows is another of those circular blue ceramic plaques. It marks the site of the Cato Street Conspiracy.

The house with its two bedrooms is now a Grade II listed building. It was on sale in 2020 for £1.4 million. Contemporary engravings, however, show a far different place. In one, the road is cobbled and dirty. Women and men alike wear high hats with peaks above the eyes. It has since moved upmarket along with the area but the street looks now much as it did then. The buildings are all there and recognisable. The archway beyond the hayloft is still there, although part of the building above it has clearly been rebuilt.

The Cato Street conspirators met in the hayloft on that top floor of No. 1a. Again, we have a contemporary illustration. It shows a small, square room with an exterior door of vertical wooden planks. It has a square peephole at eye level. To its left is a sash window with six panes to each section. To the right are two interior doors, one to the hay rack. There's a small trapdoor in the floor to the left, a central table and various other fittings, including a rack that was to serve as a step to escape through the window.

The country in those days was riddled with injustice, the conspirators said. The notorious Corn Laws kept the cost of bread high and the people short of food. The laws were intended to line the pockets of farmers and thereby keep them inclined to support the government. Those who complained were often beaten up. The Corn Laws were repealed in 1815 and then only after much bitter debate.

It was a time of revolution in Britain and on the Continent. The Peterloo Massacre was high in public memory; armed cavalry had attacked 60,000 peaceful campaigners who were calling for a more widespread vote. The soldiers charged onto a field in Manchester and killed eighteen people.

There was to be a parliamentary election for the 4 per cent of the population who could vote. The King had set off a constitutional crisis by planning to divorce Caroline rather than have her crowned Queen. The country was additionally struggling with peace after the Napoleonic wars. Some of the protesters had been dragged into those wars and then returned to find the state had forgotten them, that they were obliged to live in squalor and disease.

Some were struggling salesmen. And some were philosophers inspired by Thomas Spence, the leading revolutionary of the day. Some credit Spence for the expression 'the rights of man', the title of one of his tracts. He argued unstoppably for individual and press freedom and for the common ownership of land.

The raggle-taggle group that met at 1a with different experiences but a common grudge called themselves the Spencean Philanthropists, in Thomas's honour. George Edwards wasn't yet among them, although he was an obvious candidate. His poverty had obliged him to walk without shoes. He scratched a living on street corners by selling plaster casts he made of society figures. When things got better, he rented a small shop in Eton High Street, near Windsor.

Edwards moved back to London in 1818 and there he met John Brunt, a shoemaker who had fallen on hard times and now existed with his family on 10s a week in Fox Court. It's now a classy area of shops and offices off Gray's Inn Road but it was filthy and rat-ridden in the first decades of the nineteenth century. Brunt was a beaten-down-looking man with hollow cheeks and a flop of hair that fell over his forehead. Edwards told him that politicians ran the country and were therefore responsible for the suffering of the poor like him. If the politicians couldn't be voted out, they could be killed. That belief was his entry into the Spencean Philanthropists. And that belief was to be put into action.

On 23 February 1820, the conspirators' leader, Arthur Thistlewood, brought them together with their weapons. They planned to wait for nightfall in those stables in Cato Street and then kill the leading politicians of the day, call for an uprising, and bring about a republic. Nobody knew that the police were already watching Thistlewood as a dangerous character. And there was still more that they didn't know.

Edwards wasn't all he seemed. He had shown the group a newspaper, the *New Times*. A small item there told them that Cabinet ministers were to eat dinner together at Lord Harrowby's home a mile away at 39 Grosvenor Square. Harrowby Street is now named after him. The prospect of killing him and the other leaders of the nation excited them. They planned to knock on the door with a parcel, rush inside when the door was opened, then decapitate Lord Sidmouth and Lord Castlereagh. They hated Castlereagh in particular for his suppression of the United Irishmen, a republican group, in 1789.

The raiders would then light fires as a diversion and carry the ministers' still bleeding heads on poles on a tour of the slums. They planned to steal cannon from an army arsenal, attack the Bank of England and set up a provisional government in the Mayor of London's official residence at Mansion House.

Davidson pointed out that he had once worked for Harrowby. He said he knew the staff there and that he knew his way around the house. But a little checking would have shown that news of the dinner appeared in only that one paper that Edwards had happened to bring. Everything smelled of a plot but the conspirators were so determined that they took the bait.

They never left the stable. George Edwards' clients in Eton had included Major General Sir Herbert Taylor. Taylor was high in the Secret Service and in Eton he recruited Edwards as an informer and then an infiltrator. Everything the Philanthropists said came back to Taylor and to Lord Sidmouth, the devious Home Secretary. Edwards suggested they mention Lord Harrowby's house in the newspaper article to concentrate the plotters in one place, if they even got that far. And they didn't.

The Bow Street Runners, the forerunners of London's police force, settled into the Horse and Groom pub across the road from the hayloft and waited with soldiers from the Coldstream Guards. Then they pounced on the conspirators in a corner of 1a's upper floor. The conspirators blew out their candles and the stables fell into a noisy, smoky place of confusion and gunfire. Arthur Thistlewood stabbed and killed a Bow Street Runner, then escaped with two others. They lowered themselves to the ground by a rope ladder.

Thistlewood had the sense to run and to stay clear of his home in Stanhope Street. He holed up at 8 White Street, a three-storey house with an attic, in Moorfields. The government published his Wanted notice in the *London Gazette*, the official record, and other newspapers picked it up from there. Over the name of the Home Secretary, it offered £1,000 for information leading to an arrest. Thistlewood was, it said:

About forty-eight years of age, five feet ten inches high, has a sallow complexion, long visage, a wide mouth and a good set of teeth, has a scar under his right jaw, is slender made, and has the appearance of a military man … he usually wears a blue long coat and blue pantaloons.

A neighbour read it, recognised him and told the police his address. The Runners were there by 9 a.m. and, before he knew what was happening, Thistlewood was handcuffed to the bed in which he had been sleeping. He hadn't even undressed; there were still ball cartridges and flints in his pockets. He was questioned not just by the police but by the very government officials he had planned to kill.

A government report says:

When before the Privy Council, his dress was an old black coat and waistcoat, very much worn, and old worsted stockings. His general appearance indicated great distress; his limbs were slender, and his countenance squalid and somewhat dejected. There was nothing of agitation in his manner. He sat with his eyes fixed chiefly on the ground.

By then he must have realised the extent of Edwards' trickery. Only Edwards had seen the item in the newspaper for the good reason that no other paper had printed it. The story of the government dinner was a trick.

Edwards had also given the police the names and addresses of the Philanthropists, so that three of them were quickly arrested. There were between twenty-five and thirty conspirators. Nobody knows precisely how many. Only a few were caught. One, John George, had stopped for a pint of beer on the way and hadn't arrived. Others had held back, waiting to join in if the plot succeeded or to disappear if it didn't. Only eleven turned up in court to be convicted.

Their trial began on 15 April. Two, like Robert Adams, snitched on the others in return for a lesser sentence. Some, including John Harrison, admitted their crimes, and were sentenced to transportation for life to penal colonies in Australia.

William Davidson argued that the Magna Carta gave him the right to protest and to plot. 'It is an ancient custom to resist tyranny,' he told the court. 'And our history goes on further to say, that when another of their Majesties the Kings of England tried to infringe upon those rights, the people armed and told him that if he did not give them the privileges of Englishmen, they would compel him by the point of the sword.' His lawyer argued that planning to murder government ministers was grave but did not amount to treason. The court was not moved, and nor was it likely that it would be.

It sentenced five men – Davidson, Thistlewood, Richard Tidd, James Ings and Robert Brunt – to be hanged, drawn and quartered (less than a decade earlier they would have had their heart ripped out while they were still alive). Good crowds were common at public executions and, indeed, encouraged. But many of those who came to watch this time were expected to be sympathetic to the men's cause, or at least hostile to the actions of the government that had led to it. Such a gruesome display was sure to incite them and so the drawing and quartering were abandoned. Even so, carpenters were paid to put up barriers to keep the crowd away from the gallows, and soldiers waited out of sight, ready for action.

Thousands gathered outside Newgate Prison on the morning of 1 May 1820, those at the front having paid 3 guineas. The site is now occupied by the Old Bailey. Just before 8.30, the condemned passed through the prison's formidable iron door. A symbolic executioner's axe lay on the floor of the execution stage. This was another age and the accounts don't make easy reading.

The Traveller reported:

> The executioner, who trembled much, was a long time tying up the prisoners; while this operation was going on a dead silence prevailed among the crowd, but the moment the drop fell, the general feeling was manifested by deep sighs and groans. Ings and Brunt were those only who manifested pain while hanging. The former writhed for some moments; but the latter for several minutes seemed, from the horrifying contortions of his countenance, to be suffering the most excruciating torture.

A contemporary account, *An Authentic History of the Cato Street Conspiracy* written by George Theodore Wilkinson, said:

> Thistlewood struggled slightly for a few minutes, but each effort was more faint than that which preceded; and the body soon turned round slowly, as if upon the motion of the hand of death. Tidd, whose size gave cause to suppose that he would 'pass' with little comparative pain, scarcely moved after the fall. The struggles of Ings were great. The assistants of the executioner pulled his legs with all their might; and even then the reluctance of the soul to part from its native seat was to be observed in the vehement efforts of every part of the body. Davidson, after three or four heaves, became motionless; but Brunt suffered extremely, and considerable exertions were made by the executioners and others to shorten his agonies.

The condemned men dropped, the noose tightened and a failed plot slipped into the oubliettes of public memory. Their bodies were beheaded and dismembered by a masked man carrying a surgeon's knife. The surgeon bent the first knife on one of Thistlewood's ribs and a messenger had to be sent to the prison dining room to fetch another. The heads were shown to the crowd – the executioner dropped Brunt's – their names were recited and each was branded a traitor. And then the remains were taken away to be covered in quicklime. Only then did the tension subside and the crowd once more turned an execution into an excuse to drink and party in the street.

George Edwards also slipped into history. He sneaked away to Guernsey before the trial and the governor there arranged a new identity for him, as had happened for other government spies. He became George Parker and moved to South Africa. He died there on 30 November 1843 after writing an autobiography.

Historians still debate the significance of this uprising that never got off the ground. Some argue that if nothing else came out of it, the episode of the bent knife and the dropped head increased public disgust and that beheading was dropped because of it. James Butcher, in *The Lancet*, gives a degree of detail in the beheading that surgeons might appreciate, and then points out:

Somehow the botched attempt at assassination had been recast in the collective psyche of the working classes as a glorious attempt at revolution; the stable on Cato Street where the arrests were made and where Thistlewood had killed a policeman while trying to escape had become a major tourist attraction. So the mutilation of the dead bodies offended the crowd, who began to shout obscenities at the man in the mask as he carried out his grim work on the other four men.

Some say that public uprisings would have brought reform had the government not employed so many troops and infiltrators to prevent it. Others point out that the radicals had neither a leader nor a common purpose.

1825

DEATH IN THE WATER

Three men were working their boat along the canal that passes beneath the Edgware Road. It bounced against the tunnel wall and one was crushed. Another was injured and the third was never seen again.

Regent's Canal is a tourist attraction now. Hired boats chug along it and through the tunnel. There's no sign of the tunnel from the Edgware Road itself because it starts a short distance back and runs beneath an Italian restaurant before passing under the road. Who, crossing over it now, knows anything of three men crushed as they legged their boat beneath the ground? Or of the crookedness and embezzlement that was such a feature of the waterway?

Regent's Canal opened one sunny afternoon in August 1820. It was the sensation of the month and Londoners flocked there to celebrate an engineering and commercial masterpiece, a continuous passage through northern London and a connection of London to the rest of Britain's canals. They bought celebration coins minted for the occasion.

There wasn't going to be a tunnel at first. Then objectors made it clear that they didn't want the canal passing their house and so much cost and work were added and a tunnel was excavated. The planners told their contractor, Daniel Pritchard, to do away with a towpath. The narrower the tunnel, the lower the price, of course. Instead, horses were to be brought aboard the barges and the crew – usually a family who lived in the tiny space that the merchants were forced to leave amid the goods being transported – had to lie on their backs, raise their legs and walk themselves along the roof and through the darkness. It was called legging and it had long been familiar on other canals. It was dangerous because barges filled almost all the tunnel from edge to edge. And both they and the walls were wet and slippery.

The three men were legging through the tunnel in 1825 when the woodwork beneath them gave way. They slipped. Such was the attitude to working men's lives and what was considered the inevitability of accidents that the men's names are impossible to find. Nor are those of other men killed or severely hurt during construction of the canal and particularly the tunnel.

The tunnel, after passing beneath the Edgware Road, runs under Aberdeen Place, which will return to our history with the story of the Dambusters pilot, Guy Gibson. It runs a fraction under 2 miles with water 1.2m deep. Boat captains have to decide whose boat has access if they meet head to head because the tunnel is too narrow for both to pass at once.

The man credited with proposing the canal, back in 1802, was a sharp character called Thomas Homer, sometime merchant and persistent entrepreneur and speculator. He became the secretary of the Regent's Canal Company in 1812 and, just three years later, was found to have run off with the money. He was sentenced to transportation to Australia for seven years.

Homer had worked in the canal business before. In 1795, he was auditor of another company, the Grand Junction. In 1802, he and another lawyer, a Canadian by the name of Wentworth Brinley, proposed a canal to link Paddington Basin with the Thames. Brinley then died in January 1807. Now alone and unable to live on his lawyering, Homer ran pleasure boats, bought wharfs and traded in coal.

Business on the canal was wobbling. Work came to a halt when excavators ran into mineral seams as they dug a tunnel at Islington. The tunnel kept flooding as it passed beneath the New River. The canal company's shareholders stopped paying their dues. Some, when they were reminded, said they had indeed paid but that they'd sent the money not to the company treasurer but to Thomas Homer.

Things were getting too hot and Homer fled to Ostend, on the Belgian coast. The company wanted him back and offered a reward for his arrest. Homer moved on; he sailed to Scotland and there his escape ended. He was arrested over his breakfast in early May. He was locked into a debtors' prison and tried on 15 May at the Old Bailey. He pleaded guilty. Newspaper reports said he looked a decade older than his 54 years. He was sentenced to transportation but there is no sign that he went.

Nobody knows what happened to him. Historians have searched the registers of prisons, workhouses and mental hospitals. The only record is of the burial of a man of his name on 11 October 1838, in a churchyard in Birmingham. He is registered there as 'about 78'. You may not choose to remember him fondly but spare a thought, at least, for those who died or were injured in building his canal.

.

1829

DR GURNEY'S STEAMY DREAMS

The Tour de France is the world's biggest cycle race. It began in 1903 to promote a daily sports paper called *L'Auto*. The title suggests convincingly that its investors were indeed in the exciting new car business, but they didn't all see the future the same way. One put his money into a dream that cars of the future would walk on legs. And against that, Sir Goldsworthy Gurney's idea was altogether more sane, more logical. He predicted that cars would run on wheels and on steam, and he built one to prove it. And others built steam lorries, and steam rollers to flatten roads. So he wasn't as dotty as all that.

It was in July 1829 that Sir Goldsworthy set his pioneer steam car off along the Edgware Road, among its neighing horses and clattering carriages, to get to Bath and back. He averaged 14mph, or rather faster if you take out the time he spent stocking up on coal and refilling the boiler. That he went round Marble Arch and took the Edgware Road, which runs north, to reach Bath, a city in the west, may have been because the Edgware Road was straight and familiar from his early trials out to Edgware and Barnet. He could get out of the capital with less obstruction.

We are in an era before steam engines became common on the railways. The Rainhill Trials had yet to prove George Stephenson's idea that steam engines could pull heavy loads on rails. Gurney's invention, therefore, caused not just noise and interest but angry hostility as he advanced. His daughter, Anna, wrote to *The Times* in December 1875 that, 'I never heard of any accident or injury to anyone with it, except in the fray at Melksham, on the noted journey to Bath, when the fair people set upon it, burnt their fingers, threw stones, and wounded poor Martyn the stoker.' Gurney had to employ a guard for the rest of the journey.

Gurney built his vehicles in his garage in Albany Street, east of Regent's Park. He argued that four wheels damaged the road less than four hooves, and he put the money he earned as a surgeon into setting up the Gurney Steam Carriage Company. He wasn't the first with the idea or even the most successful as an engineer but it was he who tried to persuade a parliamentary select committee, in 1831. The committee set out in less than independent mind; its job was less to consider the utility of steam engines than to judge the nuisance they would cause and what they should be charged to use the roads (it settled on £2, twenty times the rate for horses). And it was under pressure from the makers of carts and traders in horses to ban steam engines altogether, of course.

There was also the problem that potential passengers were not excited about having to sit above the boiler. Exploding boilers in these pre-regulated days often made distressing accounts in the newspapers.

Gurney made a version that pulled a carriage to separate them from the firebox and boiler, and called it the Gurney Steam Drag. Even that wasn't reassuring. The Steam Club of Great Britain says:

> The first was sent by sea to Leith, but it was damaged in transit. It appears that this carriage was left in Scotland while Gurney returned to London for spares. He gave instructions for it not to be used, but it was transferred to the military barracks where it was steamed and a boiler explosion ensued, severely injuring two people. The second carriage may have run a service for a short time but it remains unclear whether any passengers were carried for money.

Other entrepreneurs used Gurney's steamers to replace horse-drawn stage coaches. One ran from Cheltenham to Gloucester four times a day and lasted for several months. But Francis Maceroni in 1836 wrote that:

> The many wealthy horse-coach proprietors, together with the narrow minded country gentlemen and magistrates of the district, who erroneously conceived their interests threatened by the substitution of steam power for horse, formed one of the most disgraceful and mean conspiracies against a national undertaking that can be well remembered. By means of parliamentary intrigue, and false representations, these despicable persons obtained certain local turnpike bills to pass 'the Honourable House' establishing tolls on steam carriages, which amounted to a virtual prohibition on their use.

Gurney lost his money and became bankrupt, owing £232,000. He could not compete with Parliament, vested interests and, in the end, the railways' slick organisation and their ability to carry ten times as many passengers further and more smoothly.

But was that the end? No. Gurney commercialised lighting by limelight. Theatres used it for decades and gave us the phrase 'in the limelight' for those who attract public attraction. And he invented the gas-powered Bude Light, which for decades lit the debating chambers of Parliament, the very place of his defeat. He left just £300 when he died in his native Cornwall on the last day of February 1875. The stained-glass window that the Duke of Wellington unveiled in his honour in St Margaret's Church, Westminster, next to Westminster Abbey, in July 1893 was destroyed in the war. In an explosion, just like his carriages.

1835

ROMANS AND FOOTPADS

It'd be good if the Romans had set out to reach Watling, or even Edgware. Their road is named after both, after all. But they didn't. Not in the sense that we know it, anyway. The Romans had established towns, or more likely soldiers' encampments, around the country. One was at St Albans. The Anglo-Saxons called the town Wætlingaceaster and they had a road that went there. The Romans arrived, saw their broad grassy track, and decided to use it rather than build one of their own. That's why Watling Street doesn't start where the Romans set up camp beside the Thames.

The Romans had done a good deal of marching by then. They started in Dover and followed an already ancient track that paralleled what is now the Kent peninsula to London. They then struck north to Wroxeter. It was only far, far later that the road out of London became known as Watling Street and then, less romantically, as the A5 (a number that some stretches have since lost).

And why A5? To overcome confusion. There was growing traffic on the roads in the years before the First World War but no way to guide it from Shropshire to Liverpool, say, or Southend to Bristol. Roads had names, formal or informal – the Great North Road was a prominent example – but those names changed in the course of a day's cart journey. Or roads had local names known only to individual settlements. Or perhaps no name at all. You didn't need to name the only road that passed through your parish. It was just The Road.

The government under the Liberal prime minister, H.H. Asquith, ruled that Something Must Be Done. Asquith's names were Herbert Henry, by the way, but he was always known by his initials. And so the Roads Board was set up in 1910 to define the country's busiest roads and decide which should be resurfaced with money from a tax levied on cars. The tax, paid for by annual licences, ended in 1937, when the government paid for all but the most local roads from general taxation. But the term 'road fund licence' has lingered ever since, to the irritation of many a cyclist accused of using roads 'without paying road tax'.

The Road Board started work but quickly realised that it couldn't tell one road from another either. So one of its engineers, an army brigadier called Sir Henry Maybury, stretched a map across a table and marked the six largest and longest roads radiating from London. Then he marked three more in Scotland. Each spoke from London was numbered, road 1 running north, road 2 south-east, road 3 due south, road 4 to the west, and road 5, as we have seen, to the old Wætlingaceaster and beyond. After that, roads splitting clockwise from road 1 would also start with a 1 – A10, A11 and so on – and they'd then be further subdivided into longer numbers, and so on round the country. The same thing happened in Scotland. Only tidiness gave the major highways the letter A; at first they were to have a sprinkling of letters such as H and T. Lesser roads were tagged as B and country lanes as C.

The Romans knew nothing of this and wouldn't have needed it anyway. There were only between 12,000 and 20,000 people in what they called Londinium. To give you an idea of how small their town was, the whole lot would have fitted into Hyde Park.

Nobody knows why they called it Londinium, by the way. There are suggestions that it was after an ancient called Lud, who was the son of Heli. But nobody's ever discovered who they were, even if they existed. They were in all probability just guesses when Geoffrey of Monmouth wrote his *History of the Kings of Britain*. That was in 1136, and it would be a good read if you believed that a single man could record every event since the Trojans.

Some of the legend lives, though; Lud is supposed to have been buried in what is now the City, which gives us the name of Ludgate. Or it would, were it not that we now know that Ludgate derives from *hlid-geat*, which was Anglo-Saxon for a swing gate.

The Romans ended up there, anyway, because the Thames in those days ran far wider than today, with broad banks of impassable marshes. There was a ford and one decent stretch of gravel to support a bridge. That was where the Romans crossed the water. Others followed and from that came fledgling London, enclosed by its walls.

Cities grow on trade and nowhere in Britain more so than London. Businesses set up within the walls and then outside them. Suppliers carried provisions into London and merchants brought out the transformed goods. Carts could travel only short distances on unmade roads, and so the enterprising set up roadside services to supply their drivers. That was a way for them to turn an easy penny. The drivers had to pay for those services and they had to pay a toll to use the road. But even then their worries weren't over, especially those seated high on passenger coaches. Highwaymen were likely to pounce on them from roadside woods or in darkness.

A gallows was set up in the village of Tyburn, near the start of the Edgware Road, to deal with them and other miscreants. The village name derives from 'place of the elms'. It sounds idyllic. But it wasn't for everyone. It was the site of executions from

1196 to 1783. An estimated 50,000 people were brought by cart from Newgate prison, passing down what is now Oxford Street, legend saying (it seems falsely) that they stopped for a drink on the way.

So many insisted on jeering the prisoners that a journey that could be walked in less than an hour might take three times as long. Nobody told the crowds to move along, that there was nothing to see. There was indeed something to see, and a popular belief that seeing it would keep everyone else on the straight and narrow. It can't have been wholly convincing, though: gallows grew ever larger until one could execute twenty-four prisoners at one go.

The 220 crimes that merited the death sentence in the late 1700s included cutting down a tree, stealing a rabbit warren and going out at night with a blackened face. The number of capital crimes was down to five by 1861, including murder, treason and setting fire to government dockyards, but still the bodies were hanged.

The first to meet his end at Tyburn was William Fitz Osbert in 1196. Later came Perkin Warbeck, in 1499. Described as 'vain, foolish and incompetent', he insisted he was the rightful heir to the throne. He invaded Cornwall with 6,000 men, only to find the opposition still more powerful. Strangely, the king didn't take it too personally and Warbeck got off lightly and was sent to the Tower of London. Had he not tried to escape, he would probably never have been hanged.

The last to breathe London's air for a final time was John Austin in 1783. He had pounced on a Kent labourer called John Spicer, 'cutting and wounding him … in a cruel manner'. The noose was placed on his neck as he stood on the cart. He told the crowd, always eager to hear the condemned's last words: 'Good people, I request your prayers for the salvation of my departing soul. Let my example teach you to shun the bad ways I have followed. Keep good company, and mind the word of God. Lord have mercy on me. Jesus look down with pity on me. Christ have mercy on my poor soul!' Convicts were either more articulate then or reporters tided up their words. Horses pulled the cart away and he was supposed to fall and strangle or break his neck. In fact, the rope was too slack and he took ten minutes to die.

Tyburn is now Marble Arch, the start of modern Watling Street as it runs die-straight to Burnt Oak and on to Edgware. Soon afterwards, it takes its first hill and then a bend to Elstree before continuing to St Albans. If you brave the traffic at Marble Arch, you can still see where the Tyburn gallows stood. There's a circular plaque on a traffic island at the start of the road. It reads, around its side, 'The site of Tyburn Tree'. There never was a tree, though: tree was the popular name for the wooden gallows.

But there's more. Walk along Bayswater Road and you'll find the Tyburn Convent. Its purpose since 1901 has been to pray for the 105 Catholics hanged between 1535 and 1681. The twenty nuns never leave the building, and at any time of the day at least one is praying for the victims.

1835

THE SHAME OF THE WORKHOUSE

Few places have been so awful that those nearby preferred to say they lived somewhere else. But so it was with the workhouse built on Sheves Hill field. It lay beside the Edgware Road outside Hendon, divided into strips farmed by forty-six tenants.

It wasn't a good time to be old or too infirm to work, or just unemployed. The state had recognised the plight of the poor for two centuries, but they were regarded as more a problem than a cause. A law in 1601, the Relief of the Poor Act, insisted that parishes look after them. Houseowners paid a tax calculated on the grandeur of their home. It was the start of the modern rates system. Some of those rates were used to house the destitute. The average charge across the parishes was 13s a year, which was much resented, of course. The solace was that inmates were to work in return for their meals and lodging. The buildings became known, therefore, as workhouses.

The area's first workhouse was at what is now Quadrant Close, at the south end of The Burroughs in modern Hendon. The road runs north through the suburb, starting at the busy A41 Watford Way and then curling eastwards as it becomes Finchley Lane. The workhouse opened in or may already have been open in 1735. It housed thirty-five mainly old people and the destitute. A pond stood close to it, where horses could drink. There's no sign of the building now: the site is occupied by a block of flats.

Workhouses were expensive to build and costly to run, especially since the cost came from the pockets of those who often had little sympathy for the seemingly feckless poor. So parishes banded together to build one to share, something permitted under a law of 1782 promoted by one of those striking doers of good, a lawyer and campaigner called Thomas Gilbert. His many campaigns included making sure that Royal Navy widows got their pension.

The House of Lords turned down his first plan for joint workhouses. That was 1765. But he didn't give up. The Commons considered the plight of the poor again in 1776 and Gilbert was ready with his arguments. He proposed three new laws, one of which George III dismissed as impracticable. Two of them passed, however, and, in theory, things should have become better at the larger, shared and professionally run workhouses. Sadly, they did not.

The Hendon Poor Law Union in May 1835 was the combined effort of Edgware, Harrow-on-the-Hill, Hendon, Kingsbury, Pinner, Great Stanmore, Little Stanmore and Willesden villages. Other parishes joined later and one left. Locals called their new workhouse Redhill, after the area in which it stood. It was on the north side of the Edgware Road, a little south of South Road where it now emerges as a footpath between the backs of shops and a concrete wall that has the expected attention of graffiti writers. The workhouse stood back from the main road, a fussy brick building of three storeys with fancy apexes and a church tower. Modern eyes see something closer to an institution or even a prison. Its index lists among others:

Martha Parker, having an illegitimate child
Eliza Weedon, idiotic
John Brown, old age
Ann Winfield, weak mind
Charlotte Walker, old age
Eliza Kenworth, having an illegitimate child

William Bugbee, who was deaf and dumb, was shown in 1861 to have been there for twelve years. Ann Winfield, of the weak mind, had been shut up there for eighteen years; George Pereira, also of weak mind, for fourteen. Padded rooms were added in 1890 for those considered irretrievably lunatic. The list includes only those who had been there at least five years.

The census of 1881 lists 187 occupants and their former occupation. We see that Ann Winfield had been a charwoman and was now classed as a pauper. The same went for Martha Parker. Eliza Weedon vanished between the first list and the second. So did William Bugbee. George Pereira had no occupation worth listing and was there as a pauper.

It's a sad list. It's all the sadder when you realise that the combined workhouse opened where it was because it was a good distance from the centre of the parishes that paid for it. The middle classes didn't care to see paupers and the mentally disturbed and unmarried mothers – the last an especial disgrace – and so the transgressors were banished.

Many of those who went there were illiterate or close to it. It's improbable that any of them spoke Latin. They didn't, therefore, see the irony of the notice in the entrance that promised them benevolent justice. Nor could they have reflected on the very word 'justice', which carried the common feeling that the poor had only themselves to blame and that they were to be treated as miscreants. Conditions were therefore harsh, especially under the vicar of Hendon, Theodore Williams, who was the first head of the board of guardians.

Williams had a violent temper. He flared into sudden, noisy and sustained rows. He had shares in the slave trade and that temper embraced William Wilberforce, who lived in his parish. Williams was born in Jamaica, and the Centre for the Study of the Legacies of Slavery shows him as involved in a claim for compensation for slaves the family had to set free. He was Hendon's longest-serving incumbent and his fifty stormy years at St Mary's Church are marked by a plaque there.

Theodore Williams gave Hendon workhouse a reputation for cruelty from which it never recovered. Which was why those nearby preferred to say they lived elsewhere. Williams' punishments were the severest the law allowed. Inmates were kept within the walls as prisoners, not allowed out. Breaking the rules led to solitary confinement, a diet of bread and water or a straitjacket. Some died from their treatment, and that may explain some of the gaps between the occupancy lists of 1861 and twenty years later.

Women, children and men were all accommodated separately, and women were not allowed to mix with the men, even their husbands. A song of the time, 'My Old Dutch', tells of an elderly man sent to a workhouse with his wife Sarah, known as Sal. He sings how 'We've been together now for 40 years, an' it don't seem a day too much.' Music hall audiences recognised the message. When Maurice Chevalier introduced the song in later years, he emphasised it by entering the stage dressed as a poor and elderly man. Beside him was his wife. The porter at the workhouse door sends the husband one way, the wife in another, never to see each other again. It was no exaggeration.

Children often never saw their parents again. At Hendon, however, they had a school from 1860. Its first teacher, Edward Hunwick, was a contrast to conditions elsewhere. He started a band for the boys that played for local fêtes and shows. Hunwick became master of the workhouse when it was extended in 1883. His work continued there, a capable and kind-hearted man compared to Williams' cruelty. He retired in 1893.

Attitudes towards the poor, and growing awareness of the cruelty of workhouses, changed the law. County councils took over workhouses as hospitals, and workhouses formally closed in 1930. That year, Middlesex County Council renamed Hendon workhouse, with officialdom's love of euphemism, as Redhill Public Assistance Institution. The school became Redhill Lodge, a home for elderly men.

Now nothing of the school remains. Nothing remains, either, of the workhouse. It was demolished and replaced by houses. The front of the site is now Burnt Oak register office, at No. 182 Edgware Road. The workhouse infirmary, however, was extended and became Redhill Hospital in 1927. That became Edgware General Hospital when it joined the National Health Service in 1948, although the old name persisted locally for decades. It closed in 1997, replaced by a smaller community hospital. The shame had finally passed.

1837

THE EDGWARE ROAD KILLER

They hanged James Greenacre on 2 May 1837. They called him the Edgware Road killer.

Greenacre worked by day as a greengrocer. At night, he went back to the home he shared with his fiancée or wife, Hannah Brown. They found her head in Regent's Canal. It didn't take the police long to decide that Greenacre was the immediate suspect. Word had it that he wanted her only for her money. If he could dispose of her, he could then pocket her cash and emigrate to America with his mistress, Sarah Gale. Their flight was all planned. But the police arrested them the day before they were to leave.

Hannah, who was 50, moved in with Greenacre on Christmas Eve, 1836. They were to marry but she was never seen again. Even her family never heard from her. There was no news until 28 December, when she was found by a bricklayer called Robert Bond. He was working on Canterbury Villas, in the Edgware Road. At about two in the afternoon he set off for Kilburn and came across a sack placed behind a paving stone. He moved the stone, then the sack, and discovered a pool of dried blood. He called the superintendent where he worked and, with a third person, he found that the sack held the remains of a human body.

They called the police. Constable Sam Pegler arrived. He opened the package. Inside it was a body without its head or legs. The inquest on the last day of the year, at the White Lion Inn, Edgware Road, not surprisingly recorded a verdict of wilful murder of person or persons unknown.

More of the body turned up a week later, on 6 January, the day a human head floated into Johnson's lock, on the Regent's Canal in Stepney. It was wrapped in a handkerchief. The lock-keeper, Matthias Ralph, explained:

I was called to by a bargeman, who told me there was something in the gate. I immediately went with a hitcher. I found the gates would not come to. I put the hitcher down, and pulled it along to the middle. I said, 'It is a dead dog;

ease the gate.' They eased the gate. I pulled it up, and, to my surprise, I found the head of a human being … I saw the ear first. That made me know it was the head of a human being.

The missing legs turned up on 2 February, in Coldharbour Lane between Camberwell and Brixton. A surgeon, a man named Girdwood, confirmed that the parts came from the same body. But whose? That question was answered on 20 March, when Hannah's brother identified what remained of her.

Greenacre was arrested four days later, along with 32-year-old Gale. The police found them in bed together. Their trunks, packed ready to leave for America, lay beside them. They contained some of Hannah's possessions – plus a scrap of a cotton dress of the material in which the body had been discovered in Edgware Road.

Their trial started at the Old Bailey on 10 April and lasted just two days. The jury took only fifteen minutes to decide. Greenacre was hanged by William Calcraft outside Newgate prison on 2 May, as a crowd watched. Gale was transported to Australia as his accessory.

Would they have benefited from Hannah Brown's death? In fact, not. Because the twist to the story is that she had invented the land and buildings she said she owned, to make herself more attractive as a marriage proposition. And it worked. But she had picked the wrong man.

1864

A NIGHT AT THE PALACE OF FUN

It was a palace of fun for four centuries. But then tastes changed, and at 267 Edgware Road there's now no trace.

The Metropolitan Theatre, or just the Met, was just north of where the Edgware Road is now sliced by the 2½ miles of the Westway bypass. It brought the greatest acts of the age to thousands. Literally thousands, because there was accommodation for 2,800. They gasped as they filed in for the first time. They walked into a marble vestibule paved with ceramic mosaic, the dome of a ceiling ornamented like a Moorish palace. Marble walls led to the theatre itself. It had comfortable seats, four private boxes, two bars, one tiled, the other panelled in walnut with mirrors and tapestries.

There had been entertainment on the site for centuries. The White Lion pub was there from 1524. That gave way to the Grand Concert Hall in 1836 and that was rebuilt in 1862 as the Metropolitan. It opened on Easter Monday, 1864, before being revamped in 1897 by the theatre architect Frank Matcham. The list of acts engaged for the reopening night was eye-watering, even if all are unknown today. Who now has heard of Tom White and his Arabs, the Dumond Parisian Minstrels or the Villion acrobatic cyclists?

And that was the problem. The years passed and even the biggest stars became increasingly little known. Television came in the 1950s, a novelty worth watching for its own sake as well as not needing a journey in the dark and rain. The Met added a cinema screen and, like many venues, fought back by putting on more risqué acts. It tried professional wrestling, a national passion at the time. But the end was inevitable.

The curtain fell in April 1963. The last entertainers there on Good Friday included the comedians Tommy Trinder and Ted Ray, and Dickie Valentine, a fresh-faced singer with hits in the 1950s. Hundreds were turned away. One observer wrote:

The last night at the Met was a wake. A time to remember the good days and for one more time be stirred by the music and the lights. As we sat waiting for the show to begin I looked at the faces of the caryatids supporting the stage boxes. They looked as serene as ever with no indication of their pending doom. The show was great. Never better. As we sadly exited it was hard to believe this was it.

Demolishers moved in and the theatre fell in September to make way for a road widening scheme that never happened.

1868

THE FIRST CYCLE RACE

James Moore lived in Suffolk, in Bury St Edmunds to be precise. He was born on 14 January 1849. Just where has been obliterated by a supermarket. Not that he lived there long. His father and his illiterate mother, Elizabeth – she signed James's birth certificate with an 'X' – moved to Paris when he was 4. Father and son had the same first name. Moore senior worked with horses and their carts and he set up in an alley off the avenue Montaigne. It's now the swanky heart of the Paris fashion industry.

We needn't dwell on the family for long except to mention that *Jeemie*, as his friends called him, won what legend says was the world's first formal cycle race. It was held in the St Cloud park north-west of the capital, on 31 May 1868. There's a neat symmetry here because James returned to Britain to live in Hampstead, north London, and he is thought to be buried somewhere near the Welsh Harp reservoir. The symmetry is that it was at the Welsh Harp, beside the Edgware Road, that Arthur Markham won the first race in Britain – one day later than Moore. The plaque that marked Moore's success has vanished over the years but there never was one to Markham. The paths in the Parc de St Cloud are still there but nature has taken over the cycle track at the Welsh Harp.

Moore moved back to England and lived at 56 Wildwood Road in Hampstead, his last address. His grandson, John, says:

You ask me where he is buried and I have to tell you that I just don't know. The odd thing is that my father was a good story-teller but he couldn't or wouldn't tell me where my grandfather was buried. It was as if there was some unfinished business there, some sort of mix-up, something I never understood. I did hear that he may have been buried somewhere near the Welsh Harp, but I just don't know. It's a mystery.

As for Markham and his race the next day, it was Whit Monday. History has lost why the race was held, except that the licensee of the Welsh Harp pub, William

Perkins Warner, gave him a silver cup. Maybe cash, too, or perhaps Markham sold the cup, because the story is that he spent some of what he won on a coach trip to Bath. There, on 27 June 1868, he won another race, against the favourite. We don't even know the length of the Welsh Harp race nor how many took part.

We'll come back to the Welsh Harp later, why it was there and how a splendid row broke out about nudists sunbathing there. But staying with Markham for a moment, we know that he opened a bicycle shop at nearby 345 Edgware Road in 1872 and another in Station Approach, Shepherd's Bush. Both have vanished. He gave his occupation in the 1881 census as an engineer; his 23-year-old sister, Helen, described herself as a bicycle maker.

He became entangled and then cleared in a court case in 1878 about rigging races. The Lord Chief Justice scratched his head and said: 'Inasmuch as the plaintiff allowed the money for the stake to remain in the hands of Markham, after it had been arranged that the race, which originally was to have been an honest one, was converted into a dishonest one … there will be a verdict for the defendant Markham.'

He said, though, that such was the tangle that he found for the defendant but declined to grant him his costs. In simpler language, he was cleared but with many sideways glances.

The owner of the Welsh Harp, William Warner, was a local boy. He grew up at Blackbird Farm at the junction of Old Church Lane and what is now Blackbird Hill. A row of 1930s shops now stands there. Warner bought the Welsh Harp in 1858, when he was 26. It was in the wilds then and he had to entice Londoners out of London. He added a dining room as a music hall. He leased fields as gardens and sports venues, he bought the rights to fishing and boating in the reservoir. He held a steeplechase across the fields of Kingsbury, as far as Preston, another suburb. The race was famous in its day, so famous that it led the government in 1879 to ban horse racing within 10 miles of London. He advertised skating when winters were cold enough and he brought professional speed-skaters from the Fens. They attracted large crowds.

Warner died at the Welsh Harp in 1889 when he was just 56. His brother, John, took over and in 1890 plugged a balloon into his gas mains so that a Miss de Voy could disappear into the clouds and then parachute into the water. A local newspaper reported that a boy dived in to save her. A boat got to her before he did, however.

The pub declined as rival attractions emerged, such as pleasure grounds at Wembley Park. Crowds of more than 25,000 came on holiday weekends in the middle of the 1880s. By the turn of the century, though, the growing urbanisation of the Edgware Road made the reservoir much less of a country attraction and day-trippers declined. The railway station that brought them there closed in 1903.

The reservoir is still there. So is the sailing. But there are no more cycle races, no more horses, no more women ballooning into the clouds. And no trace of Arthur Markham. Except that he sounds a bit of a crook.

1868

A MAN CALLED RUDD

There's a blue plaque outside 254 Edgware Road, just south of the Westway flyover, that celebrates a man whom nobody remembers. Yet in his day he was a celebrated music-hall singer and comedian, celebrated enough that the Music Hall Guild of Great Britain and America wanted to commemorate him. His name was Austin Rudd.

Rudd was born as Arthur Rudd on 4 December 1868 and grew up in Lambs Conduit Street, Holborn. He first appeared on stage for money when he was 22. A reviewer from the *London and Provincial Entr'acte* watched him at Deacons Music Hall in Clerkenwell and called him a 'comedian of decidedly modern stamp'. Others weren't so sure. They called his style quaint or robust and commented on his odd make-up. But they all agreed on his talent and appeal.

He wrote much of his material, which wasn't always the case. In his day, many could whistle 'Sailors Don't Care' and 'She Was in My Class' even if nobody can now. He toured for forty years, not only throughout Britain but in the United States, South Africa, Australia and New Zealand. He topped the bill with Dan Leno, Marie Lloyd, Lottie Collins, Little Tich and Bessie Bellwood, on at least one occasion seven times a day. He returned after each tour to his home in the Edgware Road.

He worked until he died, aged 60, on 24 March 1929. He is buried in his family grave at St Lawrence Church, Morden. The Music Hall Guild placed the plaque at 254 Edgware Road, on 5 September 2015. And the thousands who pass it perhaps glance and wonder who he was.

1870

THE SMELL OF STEAM

There was once a man called Ian Allan. He was tall and had a forbidding manner. He had only one leg and he didn't pass his school-leaving examination. That was enough to end his dream of being the stationmaster at Waterloo, the terminus of the Southern Railway. It was the job he'd always wanted but the closest he came to the trains was the Southern's line to and from Waterloo. Which was close, because it passed near his house in Horsham, Sussex.

Allan was born there in 1922. He never stopped hoping for a job with the railway and, in August 1939, the Southern took him on to work for 15s a week in its publicity department. There he answered phone enquiries about anything to do with the railway. And he noticed that many others shared his interest in knowing which of Southern's steam locomotives was operating where. And that was when his life changed.

Allan, with some official resistance, published a booklet that listed all the Southern's locomotives and their numbers and a little about each class. He placed an advertisement in *Railway World* in December 1942, or perhaps the following month, and the post brought back 2,000 postal orders at a shilling a time. He expanded into other railway companies' areas and his fortune was made. Legions of young boys – girls rarely saw the charm – carried his books and crossed out or underlined the numbers of steam engines they had seen while hanging about on railway platforms or beneath embankments.

The real place to be was one of the dark, dirty and steamy sheds that railway companies used to fuel, service and prepare locomotives for their day's work. One of those was beside the Edgware Road. It was a little south of where it is now crossed by the North Circular Road on its way from the shopping centre at Brent Cross to the tangle of railway lines near Wembley. The sheds were out of bounds but it wasn't hard to get inside. The gates were open to suppliers' lorries and to staff who arrived there on bicycles. Trainspotters, sometimes still in short trousers, were tolerated by those who worked there or could run in and out of the locomotives when they weren't. Staff often had too much else to do to chase them.

One of those short-trousered boys, Tony Kerrison, saw the sheds as an escape from adult conversation when he was obliged to visit relatives or his parents' friends. He remembered:

> When I became bored with grown-ups' conversation (this didn't take long), I'd excuse myself and walk along the Edgware Road a short way to where a cinder track emerged from behind a small works called Carlton Forge.
>
> I'd go down the track until the jewel I sought was revealed – No. 14A, Cricklewood Loco Shed. I used to wander into the gloomy, steamy, dirty shed, which housed numerous locos, breathing in that certain atmosphere found nowhere else. I toured around the turntables and shed-roads, climbing into the cabs of various engines but touching nothing important. There were hardly any lights in there, just the occasional oil-lamp, some of which worked in the same way as gooseneck flares do as emergency runway lighting. I was about 11 years old and sometimes wore my school mac, but none of the very few railwaymen present ever bothered to question what I might be doing there.
>
> I couldn't have joined the railways as a boy cleaner, with a view to firing and – eventually – driving, because they insisted on perfect eyesight for footplate men in those days, and I was and remain rather short-sighted.

Trains running south on the Midland Railway, which eventually owned the sheds, used to end their day at Bedford. It was there that their rails finished. What the company wanted was to run into London, a project thwarted repeatedly despite much lobbying. It finally got the go-ahead in 1863, began building the line the next year, and finished its 50 miles in 1867. The first train ran into a new terminus at St Pancras in October 1868. That was built alongside the rival Great Northern station at King's Cross. To outdo the Great Northern, the Midland built a huge hotel, which is now a Grade I listed building. It took 60 million bricks and 9,000 tons of ironwork.

The hotel was, like the Midland itself, destined to last less time than the directors expected. It closed in 1935 and is now an office block. Once a symbol of opulence, it failed to match growing expectations such as private lavatories and bathrooms. The railway and its hotel were nationalised and became part of the London, Midland and Scottish region of British Railways in 1948.

What the Midland needed as it ran into London was space to maintain and fuel its locomotives and rolling stock and to marshal them into the right order. It didn't take long to find wide open country at Cricklewood. The area then was little more than farms and a few houses for the London rich. But close to the line was the Edgware Road, an excellent way to bring in supplies to build the rail yards and a road to take out whatever arrived there. And did the Midland call its station Cricklewood? No, it didn't. There was too little there for that. It called it Child's Hill instead, after a nearby village that at least had two pubs and a small brickworks.

It took less than a decade to forget Child's Hill and for Cricklewood to grow into a small town. There were train drivers, maintenance men, clerks, signalmen, and staff to look after the horses that brought deliveries. The Midland had to build a small town of houses and streets to accommodate them. The availability of workers, combined with cheap land and the transport of the new railways, brought in other companies. The Imperial Dry Plate company set up in the early 1890 to supply the growing need for photography. Handley Page opened an aircraft factory in Claremont Road, with its own airfield. Frank Smith opened a potato crisp factory in the early 1920s, adding salt in a twist of blue paper.

But the end loomed. The Midland had a history and tradition. So did the other companies. Where their lines crossed, so did their way of doing things. Many were pleased to see the end of these rival and often inefficient individual companies, each with its own rules. They were to be disappointed. Nationalisation changed little. Rather, it formalised what had gone before, even if it brought everything into public ownership. Nationalised amalgamations, such as the London, Midland and Scottish, became a tussle between traditionalists steeped in history and accountants who took a more sober view than the private companies.

More than that, 4,000 people choked to death in five days in 1952 when a combination of fog and smoke fell on the capital and stayed there. Railways that ran on coal and supplied coal to factories and millions of houses became not a blessing but a curse. Clean Air laws successively restricted the burning of coal. Trade plummeted. The railways' accountants, already worried, saw their companies' profits tumble along with the trade. And then workers, long discontent with their pay and conditions, went on strike in May 1955. There was barely a train for two weeks. And that scared rail customers into giving much of their business to the growing lorry companies that had already taken a further slice of railway income. That same year, British Railways decided to scrap steam and move to cleaner diesel and electric locomotives, both of them needing but a fraction of the maintenance, preparation and skill.

Cricklewood sheds serviced their last steam locomotive in the middle of December 1964. The end would have come even without the accountants. Factory work had become more mechanised, less dependent on muscles, but the railways hadn't. There was a nostalgic glamour in driving the trains but ever fewer people wanted to clean them, service them or shovel coal day after day on a windy footplate. The railways were a hierarchy: clean locomotives (as Tony Kerrison remembered) to become a fireman, then shovel coal for years on the way to becoming a driver. As one fireman remembered: 'I can't say precisely how much coal I shifted into the firebox for each journey – that depended on the journey and the driver – but I suppose [it] would average between two and three tons.'

In 1967, British Railways sold the houses that the Midland had built. There's little at the sheds these days to excite the heart. Small boys now are generations too young to enthuse about steam beyond the novelty of preserved and so-called 'heritage' railways. They know nothing of Ian Allan. The sheds have long come down, the smell and excitement gone. The site is used now to service not steam but electric trains. They start at the press of a button. The water poured into them is to flush the lavatories, not to boil for steam. They are smoother, more reliable, cheaper and certainly faster than the steam locomotives they replaced.

Ian Allan died in 2015, his passion unabated. He owned and operated his own private train service, the 2 miles of the miniature Great Cockrow Railway near Chertsey. It runs at up to 70mph beside his former piggery. His company changed hands in 2017, along with his beloved list of locomotive titles. Train spotters, the few that still exist, are often considered to be middle-aged men with a passion for diesels and maps of arcane parts of the network. To be called a train spotter is not always a compliment, even for them.

1900

THE BIRTH OF AVIATION

Claude Grahame-White was a playboy and, as one observer pointed out, 'frankly, a show-off'. He was prone to dress in loud suits and to wear a bow tie. He was also fond of show-off hats. He owned one of the first cars in Britain. He was born on the edge of Southampton in August 1879, and at 30 he became inspired by Louis Blériot's flight across the Channel, in 1909. He became pilot No. 6 at the Royal Aero Club, having learned to fly at Blériot's school in France. And he then turned a field in Colindale into a small but proper aerodrome.

Colindale had an electrical engineering company called Everett and Edgcumbe, in Colindeep Lane. It owned rough grazing land at the end of Colindale Avenue, which ran from the Edgware Road to where the Tube station now stands. One of the partners was Kenelm Edgcumbe. He was born in Vienna in 1873, married in England in 1906 and then lived in Aldenham, where the Northern Line would have run had it been extended after the war.

More grandly, he was the sixth Earl of Mount Edgcumbe. The family coat of arms insisted, in old French, *Au playsir fort de Dieu*, or 'to God's pleasure'.

The sixth earl worked from 1908 to 1910 to build a plane he hoped would make his name and advertise the instruments that his company produced. Sadly, his plane never flew beyond a moment here and there and it became ridiculed as The Grasshopper.

Aviation was dangerous and therefore exciting in an era when there was every chance of not getting off the ground, or of crashing back down to it when you did. *The Times* reported in 1912 that seventy-four pilots had died in Europe and America, which was a lot and even more so when you remember how few pilots there were.

Claude Grahame-White, known as Claudie, mostly saw the excitement. He bought 220 acres to turn the Edgcumbe field into something resembling an airfield. He dreamed of Colindale as 'the Charing Cross of our international air routes'. The first airmail service flew from there in September 1911. A year later he introduced an air pageant, which pulled in 500,000 people, say some reports. The pageants continued for decades. He opened an aircraft factory that was rather grander than Edgcumbe's wooden hut. Again, according to reports, he employed 3,500 people at its peak.

There was nationwide interest in 1906 when the *Daily Mail* put up £10,000 for the first flight from London to Manchester in less than a day. It's hard to calculate money over the years but Warwick and Warwick, auctioneers and therefore involved with the past, put that at more than £3 million today. Others say less.

Grahame-White wasn't the winner. That was another Frenchman, Louis Paulhan, although he did set off from Colindale. He was in the air for just four hours and twelve minutes, followed by train by his supporters, but he spent the night in Lichfield and got to Manchester twelve hours after he'd left. The *Daily Mail* had only advertisements on its front page in those days but it splashed the story across the inside in the exclusive interview that was a condition of taking part. Lord Northcliffe also owned the *Daily Graphic*, which *did* have news on the front page, and it showed Paulhan posing above the enormous propeller and rickety landing wheels.

It was all very well the money going to a Frenchman, but that wasn't going to help the paper's sales in Britain once the novelty had worn off. Grahame-White was therefore promoted as the local hero. Ever the exhibitionist, he flew a biplane over Washington, the American capital, in 1910 and stepped out near the White House, happily waiting to be arrested to add to his notoriety. The police didn't trouble him. Instead, the newspapers lauded him for his bravado.

His flamboyance showed again the day he married Dorothy Taylor in 1912. He landed on the lawn at Hylands Park, Chelmsford, in a plane he had borrowed from Sam Cody. Cody, as much a showman as Grahame-White, claimed to be the son of Buffalo Bill Cody. But he wasn't.

Grahame-White started his own flying school at Colindale and taught the author H.G. Wells, and the Suffragettes Emmeline and Christabel Pankhurst. But then came the First World War. So handy an airfield was hardly going to be overlooked and the Admiralty took over in 1916 and then, more permanently, the RAF in 1919. The Royal Air Force flew officials to Paris for the Versailles peace conference. And at the end of the war, it refused to hand it back.

Grahame-White took the RAF to court, lost, and went off to sulk in the south of France, professing no further interest in flying. He died in hospital in Nice in August 1959, rich from his property investments. Nobody knows where he was buried. Arthur Spivak, his great-niece, wrote: 'My maternal grandmother's sister, Phoebe Lee, was married to him. The strange thing is that my family knows very little about him. I have a few photos, newspaper clippings, and silverware (including some pieces from the Aeroclub of London at Hendon) but not much else.'

The RAF clung to Colindale, which it renamed RAF Hendon, and stationed fighters there during the Battle of Britain. The Luftwaffe retaliated, not infrequently hitting neighbouring houses. Flying bombs killed four members of the Women's

Auxiliary Air Force on 1 July 1944. Another flying bomb killed everyone inside a brick barrack block. The damage wasn't cleared until the war ended. The RAF took its fighters away. RAF Hendon became a ferry port for important people visiting London. The last squadron, Metropolitan Communications, left in 1957. The last aircraft to land there was a Blackburn Beverly in 1968, delivered as an exhibit for the RAF's museum.

The RAF left for good in 1987 and the airfield became Grahame Park housing estate. The RAF had built its museum next door and the Metropolitan Police took over Hendon Country Club, the airfield's clubhouse, which Standard Telephones and Cables had used briefly as a laboratory. It established its training centre there, redeveloping it in 1974 as the Peel Centre, after the founder of London's police force, the Peelers. The first cadets arrived in August 1935.

Colindale airfield and its history gradually dispersed, becoming part of the new histories of the area we know today.

1904

OF TRAMS AND TUBES

London's underground railway is the world's oldest. Builders at first avoided tunnelling and instead dug deep troughs beside or beneath existing roads. They laid the tracks and left the surface open whenever they could, covering where they had to. It was cheaper than restoring the land.

The idea of a London Underground, as opposed to simply a London underground railway, was still a long way off. Separate companies built their lines and competed rather than cooperated, at times with neighbouring stations of the same name but neither connected to the other.

The modern District and Circle lines ran trains in a loop round central London but refused to work together. The best they could agree was that one would go clockwise and the other anticlockwise. That would have worked had they agreed to accept each other's tickets. But they didn't, and so passengers who got on the wrong line had to ride not just one stop but all the way round the loop.

To this day, Edgware Road station is not one site but two. The joint Circle, District and Hammersmith lines stop south of Marylebone Road. The later and deeper Bakerloo line stops at the corner of Edgware Road with Harrow Road and Marylebone Road. They're separate on the surface but they are at least connected by long pedestrian tunnels below the ground.

All their trains stop *at* Edgware Road but none of them run *along* it or to Edgware. To follow the Edgware Road you therefore have to take quite another Tube line, the Northern.

If you confuse Edgware Road and Edgware, you won't be the first. The Northern line, shown in black on the map, is a ganglion of routes produced by merging the City and South London company with the Charing Cross, Euston and Hampstead. The City and South London opened between Stockwell and King William Street and became the world's first underground railway. The Edgware branch of the modern combined line runs to the north side of the Edgware Road, going through the network's deepest tunnel at Hampstead.

Hampstead was the implied terminus in the company's name but the line stopped further on, once it had emerged from its long tunnel, at Golders Green. Hampstead station is 58.2m below ground, the deepest on the network, should the question ever come up in a pub quiz.

Nobody could decide what to call the new combined line. Mordenware was one option, a combination of the southern terminus at Morden and the eventual northern end of the line at Edgware. It was finally named after the very stretch of the line that was never built. Northern refers not to the direction the trains take but to an ambitious plan to take it over the so-called Northern Heights to Elstree. London Transport went as far as ordering swish, modern trains to run there, only to have first the war and then planning laws kybosh the idea. The planned maintenance area near Elstree took to making Halifax bombers instead, and then London's buses. The curved supports built to carry the line were visible for decades afterwards.

Underground trains had competition on the surface. It was easier to dig rails into the road than to tunnel beneath it. Horses pulled the first trams. London had 50,000 horses on the street every day. Legend says *The Times* predicted that 'in 50 years, every street in London will be buried under nine feet of manure'. It even quoted itself in 2017 without naming the source. Surely the paper wouldn't misquote itself. The archivists looked into it. There was a leader column on the subject, they said, and even a letter from Randolph Churchill, the father of Winston. But never had it forecast horse droppings higher than a man.

The Metropolitan Electric Tramway opened a tram service between Cricklewood and Edgware on 3 December 1904. The horses were gone. The service was now electric, taking current from overhead wires. The company still had 316 trams and 54 miles of track when it was brought into the London Transport network in 1933.

Trams rarely made money any more than the railway companies did. They were losing £1 million a year in 1933, or thirty-five times as much in modern money. The last London tram ran on 7 July 1952, from New Cross to Woolwich. The network was largely taken over by trolley buses, a combination of tram and bus that also took current from overhead wires but could be steered around parked cars and other obstacles – and didn't need the rails that are so treacherous to cyclists.

Trams had a nostalgic following, more so when they were withdrawn than while they operated, but they could not compete with the Tube. The planned extension from Golders Green to Edgware was announced in 1913. That was just in time for the war, and work did not start until the early 1920s. Edgware station opened on 18 August 1924. Burnt Oak, the penultimate stop, followed on 27 October. The London Electric Railway Company wanted Burnt Oak station to be called Heath's Hill. Hendon Council suggested Goldbeaters or Orange Hill, after a farm and a nearby large house. Early Tube maps show it as Sheve's Hill, as in the site of Hendon workhouse. It finally became Burnt Oak.

But why? Just as you'd expect, really. The area had long been known as Redhill, but that had memories of the workhouse. Almost any other name would be better. Burnt Oak came from a large oak that stood since before the 1750s at the point where three parish boundaries met. As the *Hendon and Finchley Times* explained in October 1884: 'An oak tree, which had been charred and burnt by lightning, stood on the Kingsbury side of the road, marking the boundary with Little Stanmore ... The brave old oak that had stood perhaps a thousand years disappeared, and then the parish authorities put up a stone marker stating "Here stood the Burnt Oak."' Note 'the' burnt oak.

There were just two pubs, a few houses and, until 1872, a toll gate at the junction of Deansbrook Lane and the Edgware Road at which, in the 1860s, wagons paid 4½*d* and those on horseback 3½*d* to use the road.

The tram and then the railway that arrived long after the brave old oak had perished ran through open land. The Middlesex Freehold Land Society made the most of that. Reassured that it would not be tainted by the name Hendon and its workhouse, in 1853 it began building houses to sell to those of modest means. It was a business, of course, but it had a campaigning side: until 1918, only landowners could vote, so providing houses to the less well-off extended the franchise. With its workhouse and now its housing, Burnt Oak was therefore associated from the start with the less prosperous, even downtrodden.

That, as we shall see, came to Burnt Oak in a still bigger way after the war.

1908

MOVING PICTURES MOVE IN

You don't see many film stars stepping decoratively out of limousines in the Edgware Road. Fans and photographers aren't held back there by cordons. But the Edgware Road was once a pioneer in cinema. And it lost its position only recently.

Montagu Pyke was a former commercial traveller, or door-to-door, business-to-business salesman. According to his portraits, he was fond of cigars, and of three-piece suits with a matching tie and handkerchief. A watch chain closed the bottom of his waistcoat. He was prone to pose with a cigar in hand. Cinemas weren't new – there were 1,000 venues in London between 1906 and 1910 – but they were still small. Pyke went bigger. He bought neighbouring shops at 164 and 166 Edgware Road, installed a screen and projector, and called them his Recreations Theatre, later the Cinematograph Theatre.

He had watched the people passing by and concluded that 'the class of people one sees daily on the streets … would make an appreciative audience if you gave them good value and the prices were right.'

He explained in a pamphlet:

The Cinematograph provides innocent amusement, evokes wholesome laughter, tends to take people out of themselves, if only for a moment, and to forget those wearisome worries which frequently appal so many people faced with the continual struggle for existence. It forms in fact – I like the word – a diversion. It is in some respects what old Izaak Walton claimed angling to be: an employment for idle time which is then not idly spent, a rest to the mind, a cheerer of the spirits, a diverter of sadness, a calmer of unquiet thoughts, a moderator of passions, a procurer of contentedness.

He opened another venture next year further down the road, at 382–384, and called it the Electric Empire or Imperial Cinematograph Theatre. It closed with the outbreak of war. Eventually he had cinemas all over the place, including the Gala Royal at what is now an Indian restaurant at Nos 51 and 53. He sold that and the new owners showed art films, and then what would now be seen as harmless or even ridiculous sex films but were then as daring as the censor allowed. It closed in 1988.

Pyke's cinemas were independent businesses but all part of his Amalgamated Cinematograph Theatres. He founded it with £150,000 capital. He was daring as a businessman but unscrupulous. He became bankrupt in 1915, the year in which a store of flammable film caught fire and killed one of his employees. Those were the worst of his troubles but the others were as taxing: one morning in 1915, Pyke was due at three courts at the same time, one on a manslaughter charge, another to list his bankruptcy, and a third to hear a divorce petition.

He died in September 1935. He is little remembered outside the business but his name survives him at 105–107 Charing Cross Road, thanks to the Montagu Pyke bar, once his Cambridge Circus Cinematograph, the last of his ventures and the one in which fire killed an employee.

1915

STAG LANE, STAIRWAY TO THE STARS

How many pubs are called the Bald Faced Stag? Some, but not many. There's one beside the Edgware Road close to where Watling Avenue in Burnt Oak climbs the gentle hill to join it.

Back when all was rural and one year much like the last, this was all hay fields. Goldbeaters farm had more than 300 acres of them. The tradition in the nineteenth century was that on May Day, farmers from there and elsewhere met at the Bald Faced Stag for breakfast and then rode their horse-pulled carts, decked in ribbons and rosettes, in procession to Cumberland Square, in central London. There, the hay was sold to livery stables.

There was once a pub in the Edgware Road called the Load of Hay, to commemorate the fact. That, the fields, the hay, have long gone. The Bald Faced Stag is still there, though, a self-standing three-storey building topped by a model stag, the bottom storey black and the rest white. Where the Load of Hay stood, in Bacon Lane, is occupied now by Edgware Ex-Servicemen's Club.

The Bald Faced Stag looks out at the bottom of Stag Lane. The London and Provincial Aviation Company bought the land there in October 1915. Its flying school, and then its joy-riding business, ran for just four years, not even that, before the Department of Civil Aviation cancelled its licence. The four planes the company used had unusually large cockpits. They were so large that they weakened the fuselage. The planes bowed in and out when they were on the ground, let alone in the air, which must have been as disturbing to onlookers as it was to the pilots. The Air Ministry was more than disturbed; it was horrified. It wanted the planes grounded, and they were. And that was the end of London and Provincial Aviation. De Havilland bought the airfield in 1920 and designed and built more successful aircraft there before it moved to Hatfield in 1934.

It was at Stag Lane airfield that Amy Johnson learned to fly. She didn't come from the area. She came from Hull, on the North Sea, from 85 Park Avenue. She was born in 1903, the granddaughter of a former mayor. She was the first woman to fly solo from London to Australia.

Her connection with Stag Lane was that she flew off from there on 4 May 1930 in a single-engine Tiger Moth. She called it Jason, after her father's business. She landed at Croydon, on the other side of London, spent the night there and then set off for Darwin, in Australia's Northern Territory. She arrived there on 24 May, after 11,000 miles. Jim Mollison, her future husband, flew the return journey in a little less than nine days.

There's no road named after her in Burnt Oak. There's one to Mollison, though. The two married on 29 July 1932. They had known each other for only eight hours when he proposed as they flew together. Next year they flew non-stop from Pendine Sands, South Wales, to Brooklyn, in New York. From there they planned to tackle the world distance record by flying non-stop to Baghdad.

Their fuel ran out and five times they circled Stratford, Connecticut, in darkness before crashing into a ditch. They were thrown out with no more than cuts and gashes. They did make it to India, though, and in record time, in 1934 in a De Havilland DH.88 Comet.

Many of her flights were eventful but eventually one was fatal. On 4 January 1941 she left Prestwick to deliver an Airspeed Oxford to Kidlington, near Oxford. The RAF says: 'The first Oxfords were intended for all aspects of aircrew training including gunnery and had an Armstrong Whitworth dorsal gun turret fitted. The turret was removed from later versions and they were used mainly for pilot training. In addition to their main role as trainers, Oxfords were used as air ambulances, communications aircraft and for ground radar calibration duties.'

Johnson flew from Prestwick to Blackpool and slept at her sister Molly's house. The weather changed in the darkness. Snow fell off and on next morning. It rained and there were thick clouds. She could see barely anything as she sat in the cockpit but she boasted that she would 'smell her way'.

She didn't smell well. She flew well past Oxford and on to the Thames Estuary. Nobody knows what happened then. Naval lookouts said they saw a parachute appear from the thick cloud and then a plane that came ever lower before it hit the sea. The parachute, too, fell into the sea close to the barrage balloon tender *Haslemere*, off Herne Bay. Those aboard heard a woman shout: 'Hurry, please hurry!' But she disappeared under the stern of the ship and was never seen again.

Haslemere's chief officer, Walter Fletcher, dived into the sea to save what he thought was another pilot but turned out to be a leather bag. The sea is bitterly cold in January, even in southern England. He died of exposure and he was posthumously awarded the Albert Medal, awarded for lifesaving and since replaced by the George Cross.

Theories have surrounded her crash ever since, including that she was shot down – the world was at war – or that she tried to fake her own death. The most likely explanation is that she ran low or out of fuel after flying so far beyond Oxford as she tried to find her way by smell. There's a circular blue plaque in her memory at Vernon Court, Cricklewood, where she lived.

Mollison tried for a final big record. He and the French fighter pilot and eventual politician Édouard Corniglion-Molinier set out from Croydon for Cape Town in November 1936. They failed, making a forced landing just under 100 miles short of their destination. By then, Mollison and Amy had divorced. Their rivalry for the same records had overcome them.

Mollison was drinking so heavily that the Civil Aviation Authority refused to give him a pilot's licence. He moved further into London and ran a pub. There his drinking became worse. He married a Dutch woman, Maria Clasina Kamphuis, on 26 September 1949 at Maidenhead register office. They separated on good enough terms that she bought him the Carisbrooke Hotel – a temperance establishment, no longer there – in Surbiton. He died, an alcoholic, at an addicts' treatment centre, The Priory in Roehampton, on 30 October 1959. The official verdict was pneumonia.

Stag Lane was sold for housing in 1933. The airfield's last flight was by a De Havilland Hornet Moth in July 1934. Mollison Way runs from Stag Lane to Queensbury and follows the line of Stag Lane's runway. It is all that remains of a pioneering era.

1916

THE SAD CASE OF C.L.R. FALCY

It's hard to say that the Edgware Road was the cause of Roy Falcy's undoing. There were other places as well, of course, but the Edgware Road was a favourite. A writer in 1922 spoke of the scene there:

> The painted boys … to be seen in certain rendezvous in Edgware Road … You may know these places by the strong odour of scent when you enter them, and the absence of women. The sweet boys stand at the counter, or lounge, beautifully apparelled and groomed in chairs, under the wandering eyes of middle-aged grey-faced men.

Falcy certainly saw them. And appreciated what he saw.

Falcy was born in Kent in 1893. His name was Swiss, after his French-speaking father, Gustave, an auditor. Perhaps he inherited his father's gift for figures. We know that by 1911 he was at a bank in London and that he lived at the Bloomsbury House Club at 34–38 Cartwright Gardens, near Euston. It's still there, across the road from the British Library, although no longer advertising as a club. He had no idea, the day he moved in there, that he would be thrown out of the Air Force but return as a decorated hero after the First World War.

His citation for the Distinguished Conduct Medal reads:

> For conspicuous gallantry and devotion to duty. Whilst acting as pilot to another NCO [non-commissioned officer] he and his comrade performed a most daring a successful photographic reconnaissance in order to confirm information previously gained as to the working of hostile kite balloons. During operations they were heavily fired upon, and their machine completely out of control, but thanks to their great coolness and presence of mind and to a feat of great daring performed by his comrade in order to right the machine, Sjt. Falcy regained control and brought the machine back in safety to our lines.

Falcy joined a Territorial battalion of the Berkshire Regiment before the war began. In 1915, he married Eleanor Ryan, in Epping, Essex. He transferred to the Royal Flying Corps that year, qualified as a pilot in October, and was posted to No. 5 Reserve Aero Squadron. It was at the end of that year, in December, that a military court accused him of gross indecency with other men. The court heard that he had had sex with three men in a flat in Edgware Road, and at hotels in nearby Marylebone and in Oxford Street.

The scene is therefore set. But here the story takes a twist. *The Times* reported on 3 January that: 'Morris Rothfarb, aged 16, a waiter of Russian nationality, was remanded at Marlborough-street Police Court on Saturday on a charge of demanding money with menaces of Lieutenant C.L.R. Falcy, Royal Flying Corps.' Just what Rothfarb's role was, we don't know. It's reasonable to assume that he was a rent boy. In getting to know Falcy, he probably learned that he was an officer and saw a chance of extra money. He blackmailed him, knowing that revelation would see him thrown out of the army. Falcy was sure to pay.

Whatever Rothfarb's plan, it went wrong. Falcy went to the police. The police may not have liked homosexuality but they liked blackmailers even less. On the other hand, military courts almost always found defendants guilty during the war. Falcy was no exception. He was cashiered and returned to the ranks on 14 March. But in January 1917 he trained as a military pilot, went to France with 22 Squadron that May and flew reconnaissance flights on the front until September. In his FE2b he sometimes carried his mongrel puppy, Jimmie, smuggled inside his jacket.

Falcy and his observer, Roy Campbell, set out on 16 June to photograph German balloons used to direct artillery fire. The balloons were defended by anti-aircraft guns. Falcy recorded: 'Shot down: controls cut. Campbell climbed out on plane. Both got DCM.' Campbell had had to climb down a wing to its tip to right their plane.

Falcy's log book for the last months of the war lists twenty-four successful and two unsuccessful missions. One day he wrote, 'Hit in head on first show,' but he flew a second mission that same night.

France gave him its Médaille Militaire on 8 February 1919, its highest military award and second only to the Légion d'Honneur. The man cashiered for improper behaviour in the Edgware Road ended the war with honours from two countries.

He changed his name in 1925. We don't know why. A legal announcement reads:

NOTICE is hereby given, that CECIL ROY LEON ADRIAN VALLANCE, of Cranmer House, Ramsgate, Kent, lately called Cecil Roy Leon Falcy, has, by deed poll under his hand and seal dated the 23rd February, 1925, and enrolled in the Central Office of the Supreme Court of Judicature on the 12th March, 1925, assumed the name of Cecil Roy Leon Adrian Vallance, in substitution for his former name of Cecil Roy Leon Falcy. – Dated this 13th day of March, 1925.

Falcy's marriage survived until the day his wife died. He was then married again, to Mabel Bosanko, and he and his wife spent much of their lives overseas. He joined the Royal Indian Navy Volunteer Reserve as a paymaster in the Second World War and therefore had the distinction of serving in two world wars and being in all three armed forces. He died at Maidstone, Kent, in 1958, aged 65.

1924

HOMES FIT FOR HEROES

Burnt Oak was an unlikely place to build homes fit for heroes, and for those who had lived in London's rotten, dank slums. Its station opened only in 1924, at first only at weekends. The first new houses preceded it on Burntoak farm, spelled as one word. They were followed by the Canada Park estate. Its streets had airy, fanciful names for an era that favoured down-to-earth addresses named after generals and military successes. It had Vancouver Road and Columbia Avenue. South of them eight years later came the Highlands estate with cul-de-sacs named Kenmore, Argyle and Strathmore Gardens.

In 1924, London County Council chose Burnt Oak to accommodate a huge spread of houses that it named the Watling Estate, after the old Roman road. It would build them in several styles, it said, each with an inside lavatory and a garden, set in generous surroundings. The project was so revolutionary that town planners, sociologists and even plain tourists came to look. The Tube station for decades had the words 'For Watling' beneath its name on platform signs.

The way had been set far earlier, by the Housing of the Working Classes Acts of the 1890s. Those gave London County Council the power to buy land, whether the owners wanted to sell it or not, so it could clear slums and build houses in the suburbs or beyond as replacements. Lord Salisbury, who promoted the building, said:

> Thousands of families have only a single room to dwell in, where they sleep and eat, multiply, and die … It is difficult to exaggerate the misery which such conditions of life must cause, or the impulse they must give to vice. The depression of body and mind which they create is an almost insuperable obstacle to the action of any elevating or refining agencies.

Salisbury was leader of the Conservative Party. Many on his side saw him as a traitor. He was pushing the state to intervene in the established order of things. Newspapers denounced what they considered state socialism. Lord Wemyss protested that rehousing plans would strangle 'the spirit of independence and the self-reliance of the people, and [destroy] the moral fibre of our race in the anaconda coils of state socialism'. In other words, that the poor and poorly housed were better off that way because poverty was good for them. And because the doctrine of self-help was dominant – the belief that the poor were poor through fault of their own and should better themselves without the interference of others.

Years of meetings and inquiries followed. A further law was passed. And from that emerged a legal obligation for councils to build houses for the working class. And, in north London, particularly for 120,000 people living in squalid conditions in Islington and St Pancras. Their houses would be demolished and land beside the Edgware Road, on 390 acres of Goldbeaters Farm, would be dedicated to homes fit for heroes – the largely unfulfilled promise to men returning from the First World War – and for slum-dwellers.

Burnt Oak was to have 3,968 houses with gardens on an estate with churches, schools, parks and shops. The houses would be brick, wood and steel. There would be 320 flats. Statistics show there were 10.7 houses to an acre in Burnt Oak and that there were 41 acres of parks and playing fields. Only Becontree, east of London, would be larger.

Those nearby were not happy, especially in neighbouring Mill Hill. They had a leafy, tranquil existence in suburban retreat. They had bought their houses. They had been there, many of them, since the railway connected them to London in the nineteenth century. And their very history showed their quality: Mill Hill had provided two Mayors of London, William Wilberforce, Sir Stamford Raffles and Sir James Murray, who founded the Oxford English Dictionary.

Now they were to have London's working class on their doorstep. It was bad enough that this was socialist planning. More immediate was a belief that children used to rotten tenements would commit crimes – the impulse to vice that Lord Salisbury had given as the very reason to move them to Burnt Oak in the first place. The poor, argued the people of Mill Hill, were condemned by the very man who was trying to save them.

The adults would bring revolutionary politics, of course. Campaigners against Burnt Oak called Watling 'Little Moscow' and some traders made their point by refusing to serve those who moved there. The truth was that the Communist Party was unnoticeable as a branch. Two candidates who stood in 1932 attracted less than a tenth of the votes. By contrast, the estate's Conservative Association had 150 members.

The first 29,000 tenants arrived in Burnt Oak in 1927. Most voted Labour, which told those in Conservative Mill Hill all they needed to know. They saw themselves as victims. A resident complained to the *Hendon and Finchley Times* in 1927 of flowers stolen from gardens, fruit trees stripped and of language so bad that it had shocked even a local workman.

Reality was different. Watling had sports clubs and the community centre held dances and a Christmas party for children of the unemployed. Watling Week every summer had sports and social events. Bands and floats toured the streets. But interest declined. Most would have preferred a pub, but the LCC would not allow one. The nearest was the rowdy Bald Faced Stag on the Edgware Road, built long before the estate.

A report of the conservation area that Burnt Oak is now says:

Tenants moved in before schools, roads, churches, shops or any community facilities were provided. To start with, children travelled by train to Golders Green and Hendon to go to school. It seems that most people commuted to their former jobs on the Underground. Although a lot of local facilities were eventually provided, the estate was designed as a garden suburb and was never meant to be isolated from the rest of London. Watling Estate was a very alien environment for many of the first residents. One reminiscence of the early years explains how in 1928 'there was nothing but bricks and mortar and acres of mud. The main thoroughfares … were narrow lanes – little more than footpaths and cart tracks in part.'

The first doctor had to live in a caravan until his house was ready. The houses were larger and better equipped than the tenements left behind, there was space for gardens, parks and playing fields, but in comparison people felt isolated and lonely. Early residents complained of the quiet, the lack of facilities and the cost. Although the houses were subsidised by the LCC, rents were often higher than people were used to whilst the cost of travelling to jobs further into London and of acquiring furniture often resulted in real hardship.

The Tube no longer announces its station as 'For Watling'. Burnt Oak, once feared as Little Moscow, is more usually referred to now as Little Romania. More of that later.

1927

THE NEWCOMERS

It is flattering that the Edgware Road should be called that because there was nothing at Edgware for centuries. Historians are convinced that the name comes from Ecgi's Weir. He was a Saxon, it seems, but there's no clue who he was or why his weir was thought worth marking. The Romans passed through as well, with their fancy for line-straight roads, and they made pottery at Brockley Hill. That's the first rise worth mentioning after the Edgware Road leaves Marble Arch, and it's where the old road turns gently right to St Albans. Ecgi's Weir is in an Anglo-Saxon charter of around 975 but it didn't make it to the Domesday Book.

It's said that medieval pilgrims travelling from London to St Albans stopped at Edgware to rest. That was in 1375, so there were inns and perhaps more there then. Edgware by the 1600s had grown to 120 people. They included butchers, brewers and a seller of charcoal. The church was rebuilt in 1764, by which time Edgware was becoming an important coaching halt, and a starting point for some services to London. Several inns were established and Edgware held fairs in the eighteenth and nineteenth centuries.

The place wasn't without its upsets. Thomas Disney, the curate in 1586, was branded an 'old and ignorant' man. Another curate, John Whiston, was sent packing in 1644. Richard Swift replaced him in 1656 and was equally sent on his way in 1660, after which he founded a boarding school for Quakers at Mill Hill. It seems not to have lasted long.

The much later Jewish community also had its divisions. The *Jewish Chronicle* reports that the 150 members of Kol Nefesh synagogue broke away 'after a split within Edgware Masorti over the sight of women in tallitot [prayer shawl]'. God's peace did not, it seems, extend to the leaders of his local flock.

This quiet if occasionally disputatious life was disturbed after a while only by the traffic on the Edgware Road, for which there was a toll gate where the Army Reserve Centre now stands. Nine coaches a day passed through Edgware by the end of the coaching age. But far from thriving, the population fell in the middle of the nineteenth century. Surrounding areas grew but Edgware slipped back. And down and down it went until the 1880s.

Things changed a little with the opening of a tram line from 1904 but recovery and finally growth did not happen until the Underground stretched out from Golders Green to Edgware in 1924. Six years later, Edgware had a shopping centre and suburban streets. Factories moved out from central London, including the musical instrument makers Boosey and Hawkes, in the 1930s. The company set up in Deansbrook Road, on the approach to Burnt Oak.

The Edgware Way bypassed the town to the north from the middle of the 1920s and, in pre-planning days, builders bought land on each side. John Laing made a start in 1936. Work would have romped on had it not been stopped by the war and then by planning laws and the imposition of a Green Belt to prevent London's endless devouring of the countryside.

This new suburbia had leafy street names such as Hillcrest Avenue, even though it barely rose, and Priory Field Drive, to celebrate what had been there before the builders dug it up. Further north, a builders' flight of fancy led to roads running in semi-circles around each other so that to follow any of them brought you back to close where you'd set off.

The one remaining link to the past is Clay Lane, an unsurfaced track from the sixteenth century that runs north towards another new estate, the town of Borehamwood. At its end is Edgwarebury cemetery, a Jewish cemetery in four parts that has been there since 1972. It's shared by neighbouring synagogues.

It brings us to another aspect of this last town on the Edgware Road and the Northern Line. It's the size of the Jewish population. One count says there were precisely 7,803 Jews in Edgware in 1963. That's a fraction less than 40 per cent of the population. The 2011 national census says that of those who identified themselves as religious, 5,500 were Jewish. But why so many? And why should one of Europe's largest synagogues stand not in London's East End or any other traditionally Jewish area but alongside the Edgware bypass? Why should the neighbouring Orange Hill grammar schools on the approach to Burnt Oak now be Jewish schools?

Legend says the Barnett family was the first to move, in 1927. Legend doesn't, though, say why or from where. The story also falls short in that it says that this first family found enough other Orthodox Jews to start the Edgware Hebrew Congregation. Perhaps they came later. They met in members' houses, then in a hall in Canons Park, on the edge of Stanmore. They advertised for a rabbi in the *Jewish Chronicle* in 1931 and appointed Saul Amias. He stayed until March 1975, a residency broken only by working as a forces' chaplain during the war. His work included establishing Rosh Pinah School.

A property developer then gave the community land in Mowbray Road, close to the bypass, and a synagogue was consecrated there on 2 September 1934. The congregation went there until the giant synagogue was built on the other side of the Edgware Way in 1957.

Edgware Way still carries traffic from the Apex Corner junction with the A1, around the side of Watford and on to the new town of Hemel Hempstead and the county town of Aylesbury. It was overshadowed for decades by the older A1, which ran to Newcastle and beyond, and it's now overshadowed in scale by the M1 motorway.

The M1 originally ended at Berrygrove roundabout on the Aylesbury road outside Watford. The transport minister, Ernest Marples, warned that 'on this magnificent road, the speed which can easily be reached is so great that senses may be numbed and judgment warped. The margin of error gets smaller as speed gets faster. New motoring techniques must be learned … Take it easy, motorists!'

Three thousand drivers tested the road in its first hour, some at Marples' frightening speed. There was no limit and nor was there a central barrier to stop cars veering into oncoming traffic. The M1 stopped at that roundabout for years while planners tried to find a way to bring it into London. The Highway Development Plan had drawn a circle of fast roads surrounding the capital as far back as 1936. Other than among those whose houses would be demolished or their lives polluted by exhaust and noise, the plan was welcomed as a leap into modernity. The report was so popular that one of the authors, Sir Edward Lutyens, found they had sold out before he could buy one. Not until 1986 was the M25 opened, London's orbital motorway.

Back in Edgware, streets of social housing emerged in the 1950s alongside the private estates of John Laing's period. They reached from Laing's houses as far as the London to Manchester railway line, often despite the protests of those who followed Mill Hill's lead and saw council houses as lowering the elegance of the area, and their children doubtless as awful as they were forecast to be on the earlier Watling estate.

Now the houses and the railway are skirted by the M1 as it makes its smooth way north in one direction and its crowded and convoluted way in the other to fizzle out in Golders Green. Should the six-minute drive north from London prove taxing, there is a service station at Scratchwood. Scratchwood is now far better known than Edgware and, incomprehensible to many, is more attractive for an evening out. It opened in 1969, and as well as burgers and slot machines, it has a hotel for those who find it so delightful they want to extend the experience.

Sadly, Scratchwood's name again reflects builders' enthusiasm for naming places after what they have destroyed. Where the Middlesex forest once spread, there is now just housing and traffic. Scratchwood service station is all that remains.

1929

THE BIRTH OF TESCO

Burnt Oak Tube station stands in Watling Avenue. The road runs flat from the old steam station in Bunns Lane at the Mill Hill end, then climbs to the Edgware Road after crossing the Silkstream near Burnt Oak station. It was on that slope that the first branch of Tesco opened in September 1929, at No. 54. The site is now occupied by a Halal food shop. Tesco moved soon afterwards to a larger plot at No. 9, now the site of Superdrug, a retail pharmacy.

Jack Cohen may have dreamed but he could never have foreseen that his first shop would develop into Britain's biggest supermarket chain. He started, after all, with just a market barrow. He was born in London's East End, in Whitechapel, in 1898. He had a broad face that tapered to a long chin, and features that wouldn't be remarkable except for heavy eyelids and a slightly sneering mouth. The *Jewish Chronicle* described him as 'not, by any measure, a good-looking man'.

His parents were from Łódź in central Poland. They called him Jacob Kohen. He called himself Jack, and later, Jack Cohen. A blue plaque stands outside 91 Ashfield Street where he grew up. He worked at first as a tailor, with his father, Avroam, but they fell out when Jack opened a market stall, a move his father saw as below the family. Tailoring was a profession; selling from a barrow was not.

Long before the barrow, Cohen made canvas for flying balloons and aircraft wings in the Royal Flying Corps during the First World War. Posted first to France and then to Palestine, he was shipwrecked in the Mediterranean by a German mine in 1917. The ship sank in seven minutes and 209 soldiers, nurses and even the ship's captain drowned.

The nation gave Cohen £30 when the war ended and he spent it on tea to sell from a stand in Well Street in South Hackney. In fact, the money went back to the government because the tea was surplus stock at the NAAFI, the government's military supplier. Cohen took £4 on his first day and made £1 profit. He worked out that he could sell more tea if he distinguished it from others by giving it an exclusive name.

So he called it Tesco. The first three letters came from Thomas Edward Stockwell, the Islington businessman who supplied the tea, the last two letters from Cohen's surname. Tesco then gave its name to the first shops in Burnt Oak.

Why Burnt Oak, 10 miles from South Hackney? It's not clear. Maybe land and buildings were inexpensive. The Tube had been open only five years. It was decades away from being the commuter station it is now. On the other hand, London County Council was about to build an enormous garden estate to be populated by the inner London slum-dwellers that Cohen knew.

He chose Burnt Oak and arranged to have a sign across the shop that boasted 'Tesco Stores Ltd, the modern grocers' and piled Tesco tea in the window with whatever other tinned goods he had to sell. It went well; two years later he built a headquarters and warehouse at Angel Road, Edmonton, also in north London.

The first shops were traditional. Supermarkets were still a distant, American idea, glimpsed perhaps in American films popular during and after the war but far from the dowdy 1950s of British rationing and shortages. Cohen went to America in 1946, saw how things were done, but returned unconvinced that Britain would accept self-service. It was his son-in-law, Hyman Kreitman, who persuaded him.

Tesco opened its first supermarket 10 miles further up Watling Street, in St Peter's Street, St Albans, in 1948. There are now 2,834 of them, or twice as many if you count franchise shops and those in Ireland. Together they make Tesco the third largest retailer in the world by gross revenue.

Cohen died aged 80 in 1979. His operating motto was 'pile it high and sell it cheap'. Less publicly, he used the initials YCDBSOYA on his tie pin – 'you can't do business sitting on your arse'.

He is buried in the Jewish cemetery in Beaconsfield Road, Willesden. His gravestone is topped by a line of Hebrew and followed in gold italics by 'Sir John Edward Cohen, 6th October 1898 – 24th March 1979'.

In birth he had been Jacob, in business he was Jack and now in death, and knighted, he is Sir John.

Below him on the same stone is Lady Sarah, his wife. Again there is a name change; she was indeed Sarah but she had been known all her life as Cissie. She died in 1989. Her name survives in the Lady Sarah Cohen House in Friern Barnet, a Jewish charity that is part of the National Health Service.

1930

THE NUDISTS OF THE WELSH HARP

The Welsh Harp is just after where the Edgware Road crosses the capital's inner ring road, the North Circular. It's a reservoir created by the damming of the Brent and Silkstream in 1834 to provide water for the Grand Union canal. The planners called it the Brent or Kingsbury reservoir but local people knew it by the name of a pub that once stood there. Now the Ordnance Survey has followed suit.

The Harp and Horn was renamed the Welsh Harp by 1803 and the Midland Railway copied it when it built a station beside it. Neither the pub nor the station are there any more. The station was pulled down in 1903 and the pub was demolished in 1971 in plans to extend the M1 motorway into London.

The Midland thought the station would appeal to Londoners escaping the capital. *The Penny Illustrated*'s 'Holiday Notes' in 1869 reported that 'a holiday at Hendon is quite a recognised cockney treat'. Locals had bathed there since the reservoir was created, something we know from church records. They report that four teenage boys drowned there in the summer of 1835, one while trying to rescue the others.

The reservoir is crossed by a road called Cool Oak Lane. A path from there led down to Sandy Cut. It's hard to say just where that was but it's probably now a car park. A local man was happy to allow sunbathers and swimmers to enjoy themselves there. The poor bathed dressed when they could but naked when, more likely, they didn't have clothes to get wet. Word spread, and by 1930 committed naturists joined them.

And it was then that the row started. A couple spotted them as they walked home from church. And in the tradition of the times, the man wrote to the local paper:

Why is naked sun bathing permitted in the Welsh Harp Reservoir without some enclosure, where sexual maniacs can perform out of view of the more respectable members of the community? On Sunday evening last my wife and myself were walking across from Old Kingsbury Church to Edgware Road, and were half-way over when we came upon a bunch of stark naked men hanging around the water side. Hardly a pleasant sight for a man to have to pass with his wife.

He added: 'Even the lowest type of native covers himself, and were coloured men committing this offence half the folk in Kingsbury would want them lynched.' More letters followed. The racism in 'were coloured men committing this offence' is clear. Lawrence James, a historian, writes: 'Prejudices mingled in the outcry of onlookers who were horrified to see "white girls" swimming close to two "very dark-skinned men".'

It was all that local people could hope for. Now they could gawp and be offended at the same time. Hypocrisy abounded. Two days of fracas in the quiet days of summer made the national as well as the local papers. Crowds turned up to bait and beat forty bathers. The local paper reported: 'When the sun bathers began to dress, the crowd surged among them and angry words were followed by blows. The bathers' clothes were scattered and trampled underfoot while the pressure of the crowd was so great that people were pushed into the lake.'

The *Daily Telegraph* reported:

A mob attacked a party of sunbathers, twelve of whom were women … The sunbathers, some of whom wore no clothes at all, were beaten, but no one was seriously injured. The crowd objected to them because children were watching the proceedings. Further scenes were prevented [the following day] by the presence of four policemen, but despite this protection impolite remarks were flung at members of the cult by a huge crowd which had gathered to watch them. 'The police told the crowd that this was private land and they had no right to interfere,' Captain H. H. Vincent, secretary of the Sun Ray Club and the New Life Society, stated yesterday.

Note the word 'cult'.

The police appeared but to maintain order, not to clear the naturists away. The sunbathers, they agreed, were on private land and not visible from the footpath. Anyone offended had gone out of his way to be offended. Harold Vincent told reporters: 'We put up notices warning people that sun bathing is taking place but they will come and stare at us, and some of them even take photographs. Dress or undress is optional with us. The objectors are ignorant people, with whom it is useless to argue.'

Willesden councillors visited the site and told the sunbathers to leave within the hour. The *Daily Telegraph* reported:

Selecting a mahogany coloured man, wearing as near to nothing as was possible, Councillor Hill on behalf of the council, delivered him the edict.

'What is the nature of your objection?,' the mahogany-coloured man asked.

'I object to you particularly,' Hill replied.

The sunbathers asked Kingsbury Council – one newspaper rendered it as 'Kinksbury' – to rent them land beside the reservoir. But 'after very careful consideration', it decided not to, since 'the deputation stated there would be no costumes worn and there would be intermingling of sexes'.

Evelyn Waugh, the writer, doubted the value of sunbathing and complained that 'people will believe anything they are told by "scientists" just as they used to believe everything they were told by clergymen'. Of the Welsh Harp, he said, the naturists could have been more tactful but the fault lay with protesters who had 'assemble[d] in a large crowd at the one place where they know they will see the very thing which displeases them'.

Never again did nudists bathe en masse beside the Welsh Harp.

1935

JAQUES THE PIANO MAN

Jaques and Erna Samuel could see the way things were going. It was 1935, in Austria. A troubled time.

Things didn't look good, and so Jaques and Erna fled to London. Language was a problem, of course; nobody they knew in London spoke German or, possibly, Yiddish. But Jaques had a trade he could continue. He didn't need another language to tune pianos and to sell those he reconditioned.

He set up business in his front room in Notting Hill and then in 1972 moved to 142 Edgware Road, six streets north of Marble Arch. By the time he sold his business in 1965, he was supplying pianos for the BBC and to hundreds of individual customers. It's said that most students studying music in London rent their instruments from Jaques Samuel Pianos.

Jaques fell ill in the 1960s and died in 1965. The business has been managed since 1996 by Terence Lewis, the former piano buyer at Harrods. He spoke in an interview of his strangest customer:

We had to supply two grand pianos for flamenco dancers to dance on for one night in Barcelona and had to create fake lids as the pianos can't usually withstand the weight of people dancing on them, let alone in stilettos! I guess they couldn't find anyone to make this happen in Spain so they came to us.

Another odd request was for a ballet performance. We created a piano that looked like a bed for two ballet dancers in *Cry Baby Kreisler* by the Royal Ballet, which premiered in 1996.

Jaques could never have guessed.

Emma Hamilton, seen here in a theatre role, was a beauty of the day and mistress to Admiral Nelson. But all went wrong and she died an addict and in poverty.

Britain's government would have been overthrown if a bunch of idealists hadn't been revealed even before they set off from this first-floor apartment in Cato Street.

Arthur Thistlewood,
Cato Street conspirator.

The tunnels of the Regent's Canal could be fatal to the bargees who walked their vessels through the darkness. The canal itself led to a financial manhunt.

Sir Goldsworthy Gurney dreamed of travel by steam, a dream that made him bankrupt. But he did give us the phrase 'in the limelight'.

Sir Goldsworth Gurney's carriage could hardly have been more conspicuous as it steamed along the Edgware Road.

Hundreds died on the gallows at Tyburn, in modern Marble Arch. Less well known is the nearby convent that remembers Catholics who breathed their last there.

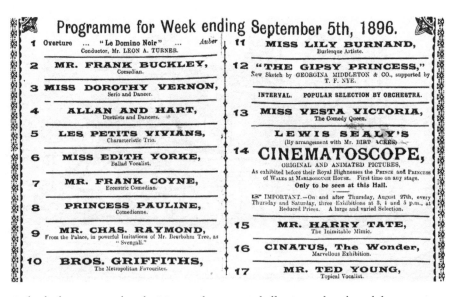

Programme for Week ending September 5th, 1896.

1. Overture ... "Le Domino Noir" ... *Auber*
   Conductor, Mr. LEON A. TURNER.

2. **MR. FRANK BUCKLEY,**
   Comedian.

3. **MISS DOROTHY VERNON,**
   Serio and Dancer.

4. **ALLAN AND HART,**
   Duettists and Dancers.

5. **LES PETITS VIVIANS,**
   Characteristic Trio.

6. **MISS EDITH YORKE,**
   Ballad Vocalist.

7. **MR. FRANK COYNE,**
   Eccentric Comedian.

8. **PRINCESS PAULINE,**
   Comedienne.

9. **MR. CHAS. RAYMOND,**
   From the Palace, in powerful Imitations of Mr. Beerbohm Tree, as "Svengali."

10. **BROS. GRIFFITHS,**
    The Metropolitan Favourites.

11. **MISS LILY BURNAND,**
    Burlesque Artiste.

12. **"THE GIPSY PRINCESS,"**
    New Sketch by GEORGINA MIDDLETON & CO., supported by T. F. NYE.

    INTERVAL. POPULAR SELECTION BY ORCHESTRA.

13. **MISS VESTA VICTORIA,**
    The Comedy Queen.

14. **LEWIS SEALY'S**
    (By arrangement with Mr. BIRT ACRES)
    # CINEMATOSCOPE,
    ORIGINAL AND ANIMATED PICTURES,
    As exhibited before their Royal Highnesses the PRINCE and PRINCESS of WALES at MARLBOROUGH HOUSE. First time on any stage.
    Only to be seen at this Hall.

    ☞ IMPORTANT.—On and after Thursday, August 27th, every Thursday and Saturday, three Exhibitions at 3, 4 and 5 p.m., at Reduced Prices. A large and varied Selection.

15. **MR. HARRY TATE,**
    The Inimitable Mimic.

16. **CINATUS, The Wonder,**
    Marvellous Exhibition.

17. **MR. TED YOUNG,**
    Topical Vocalist.

Only the best appeared at the Metropolitan music hall as its peak – though how many acts are remembered now?

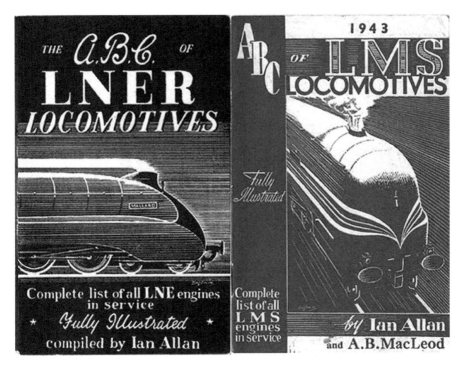

Ian Allan's lists of locomotive numbers thrilled schoolboys until diesel took the place of steam.

A show-off is how even his friends described the aviator Claude Grahame-White. As well as his flying exploits, he dreamed of turning Colindale airfield into an international airport.

Montagu Pyke was a pioneering cinema entrepreneur – and a frequent visitor to the law courts.

Amy Johnson perished while flying by sense of smell, as she put it. Her dissolute husband is remembered in the name of a street beside Stag Lane aerodrome.

Jack Cohen, founder of Tesco supermarkets.

Such was the influence of the Watling Estate in planning circles, and the number of visitors to it, that for years Burnt Oak Tube station was identified as 'for Watling'.

Jack Cohen rose from a single stall in an East London market to the head of Britain's largest supermarket chain. His motto: You don't do business sitting on your arse.

Britain's fate came close to depending on the long corridors dug beneath Neasden at the edge of the Edgware Road.

The bravery of Guy Gibson and his crews was celebrated in *The Dam Busters*.

Commercial sex was rampant in Britain's cities during the war. Not least in London, where street after street brimmed with brothels or lone prostitutes.

Britain wakes to the news of the Great Train Robbery near Leighton Buzzard in Bedfordshire.

Agent Zigzag, an extraordinary story of crook turned conspirator to foil the Nazis.

1935

A LITTLE PLACE OFF
THE EDGWARE ROAD

It's not one of Graham Greene's best tales but it was in his debut volume of short stories, *The Basement Room*, published in 1935. Greene was self-effacing, saying in a modest preface to a later edition: 'I am only too conscious of the defects of these stories … [It] is an exacting form which I have never properly practised.'

One review of 'A Little Place Off the Edgware Road' nevertheless calls it 'a masterly handling of the genre, combining many of Greene's own spiritual and religious concerns with a stylistic quality akin to that of Edgar Allan Poe at his most powerful'.

The story is of a man called Craven, an author of crime fiction who can think of nothing to write. Troubled by that and by memories of his wife and child, he wanders the streets around the Edgware Road until he comes upon a cinema advertising itself as the Home of the Silent Film. He goes in, as much to get out of the road as to watch films. He settles in the darkness of the auditorium and tries to understand the film.

He is not alone. The bearded man next to him whispers in his ear of a Bayswater Tragedy. The two shake hands and part. Craven realises the man's hands are sticky and he finds a smear on his hand. The man he has been sitting beside was the murderer.

Craven panics and calls the police. But the police tell him that they already have the murderer. What they don't have is the dead body.

Things become darker still. Craven realises he has been sitting next to not the killer but the corpse. A corpse that spoke to him and shook his hand. He screams and refuses to believe that he has become mad.

But, says a reviewer, 'we know that he already has'.

1937

THE SPIES AND THE SHAPELY BLONDE

Every spy story should have mysterious foreigners, a spymaster, a blonde, some well-meaning traitors and a smattering of sex. This one has them all.

We start at Forset Court, which is on the right of the Edgware Road, four turnings after leaving Marble Arch. It's a solid, brown block of flats with a row of shops on the ground floor. A one-bedroom flat there was priced at £550,000 in 2023 with annual service charges of £5,800. It was there that Mr and Mrs Stevens lived or, sometimes, Mr and Mrs Stephens.

Those weren't their real names, of course. In reality they were Willy and Mary Brandes. Or they said they were. In fact – and yes, this is getting as complicated as spy stories are supposed to be – Willy Brandes was actually Mikhael Borovoy, a Soviet agent who had escaped from Canada after being rumbled for irregularities in his passport. On arriving in London, the couple called themselves Brandes.

The couple spoke to each other in French, at least in the hearing of others. Borovoy was confident but noticeably hesitant when he spoke. He had 'very thick, short fingers', said the blonde in the case. The Soviet embassy hadn't registered them as diplomats; they were what the trade called 'illegals'.

Moscow sent them to London to bring life to a spy ring at Woolwich Arsenal, a huge military factory beside the Thames. They and their controllers were interested in new 14in guns for King George V-class battleships. They could be fired every thirty seconds. Moscow was interested because a naval treaty in 1936 limited the number of battleships and the size of their guns. Britain, France and the United States were allowed to go from 14in to 16in guns if Japan refused to sign the agreement, which looked likely.

What Moscow wanted to know was whether the Royal Navy was already building that 16in gun. It didn't trust the British, who had once invaded Russia in the hope of stopping the communist revolution and had already attacked Murmansk and Archangel. A battleship with a 16in gun could shell Leningrad from too far out to sea for the Soviets to respond. It wanted to see the plans.

Arms arsenals were an obvious attraction for spies, especially those before the war who believed the idealism of a workers' paradise that the Soviet Union promoted and who resented the monopoly of power held by capitalist politicians. The spies at Woolwich were Percy Glading, Albert Williams, George Whomack and Charles Munday. Their ages ranged from 22 to 54.

Williams was an examiner in the armaments area, Whomack an assistant foreman working on naval guns, Munday an assistant in the chemists' department. Glading had been expelled from the Arsenal because of his communist opinions. He became a national organiser for the British Communist Party, enthused the others and organised the ring.

What neither the Borovoy couple nor the Woolwich communists knew was that they and their party had been infiltrated by a Miss X, as she was called at the initial hearing, 'a young and pretty blonde'. Or as *Time* reported: 'This slim, bob-haired blonde, English to judge from her accent, arrived curvesomely sheathed in clinging black, and kept shifting her handsome fur piece with the sinuosity of Mae West, as she testified before a bug-eyed judge.'

Miss X was in fact Olga Isabelle Gray, a woman born into a far-right family in Lancashire. She was at a social gathering of Birmingham Conservative Party when a woman called Dolly Pyle asked her: 'I say, old thing, have you ever thought of working for the Secret Service?' Pyle was a secretary at MI5 who looked out for potential recruits. Gray was sent to meet a man who introduced himself as Captain King. She became a spy, agent M/12. Maxwell Knight – 'M' – was penetrating the communist party. He had already so successfully penetrated the British fascist movement that he became its intelligence director. He wanted her to infiltrate the Communist Party.

Henry Hemming, Knight's biographer, says she:

started to flourish among the well-meaning progressives of the Friends of the Soviet Union ... One of those communists who heard about Olga's secretarial prowess was Isobel Brown, a tiny political activist from Newcastle upon Tyne who had been jailed previously for making an inflammatory speech to a group of British soldiers. More recently, the Home Office has described her as an important communist 'engaged in some particular form of revolutionary activity' and suspected her of having recently gone to the Soviet Union for a 'special course of instruction.' But they had no further details.

In August 1932, that looked set to change when Isobel Brown offered Olga Gray a part-time position at the two organisations where she herself worked. Both were communist fronts with a more direct connection to Moscow than the FSU.

Harry Pollitt, the British Communist Party's general secretary, was so impressed that he asked her to travel to Paris with him. They may have had an affair there.

In Paris on 6 June 1934, they were to meet Percy Glading, a witty and genial man with lank hair and prominent lips whom MI5 considered one of Britain's most dangerous communists.

MI5 knew that Glading had been a regular caller at the Borovoys' flat. They also knew, because Gray was sufficiently trusted that she was there when it happened, that documents from Woolwich Arsenal were taken there and photographed, clumsily, it seems. Gray passed on to MI5 that Glading was to meet a man at Charing Cross station to collect more documents. MI5 were waiting. They arrested him and then Williams, Whomack and Munday. They were convicted and jailed in March.

They didn't prosecute the Borovoy couple because their nationality, possibly Romanian, perhaps Russian, maybe even Canadian, would have embroiled them in too many diplomatic problems. MI5 or the police could have arrested them whenever they chose because of their false passports. They could have done it as they passed through emigration controls at Dover. They didn't. They had the spies; the Borovoys, they concluded, were just the messengers.

The couple left Edgware Road by taxi in November 1939, loading their luggage as MI5 watched them unseen. They watched again as the couple boarded the Paris boat train at Victoria station. It was after that they lost touch. Stalin called back thousands, perhaps 20,000 or more of his overseas agents. Many went to the Lubyanka jail and were never seen again. The same probably happened to the spies of Forset Court.

1939

THE SECRET CONTROL CENTRE

It's hard to imagine the country being run from Dollis Hill. It's one of those anonymous 1930s suburbs beside the Edgware Road that only the people who live there can find on a map. And yet there, down below a modern housing estate, is the command centre that would have replaced the Cabinet War Rooms in Whitehall had they been destroyed.

The centre's code name was Paddock and it's still there, a busy layout of damp corridors lined by water pipes and electrical cables, the walls covered with the shallow white shiny tiles you still see in unimproved Underground stations. As at later centres built in case of a nuclear war, Paddock had a BBC studio from which Churchill and others could address the nation. The place would have bustled with worried-looking men and their secretaries from the War Cabinet and the heads of the three services.

Civil servants could see as early as 1937 that the government might have to move to the north-western suburbs. That centre would in turn have relief centres in rural western England. It was in western England, too, that the BBC would be, and to a large extent actually was, evacuated. The Imperial Defence Committee wanted to move out west and be done with it. Instead, the country got four underground bunkers in London: the Admiralty at Oxgate Lane, Cricklewood; the Air Ministry in Harrow; the Army in Twickenham. Dollis Hill would be the central command, on the site of the Post Office research laboratories. The choice was risky because the research station was already an obvious bombing target.

Digging started at the beginning of 1939, by which time even major earthworks attracted little curiosity. It was best not to ask. Many assumed they had to do with the laboratories. The plans called for a sub-basement with a concrete roof 5ft thick, above it a larger first basement protected by another 3½ft of reinforced concrete. Building was complete in June 1940. Oddly, there was nowhere to sleep; the plan was to commandeer sixty flats nearby for senior staff and secretaries. Churchill wanted two flats to be knocked into one as a personal suite. Everyone else would have bunks in local schools.

The centre was lightly staffed throughout the war, just in case. Churchill didn't want to move, but he visited Paddock at the start of the Blitz. The War Cabinet met there to try it on 3 October 1940. Planners called it Paddock, picked for no reason from a book of code names. And they weren't impressed. Or Churchill wasn't, anyway. He declared it 'quite unsuited' and that the 'War Cabinet cannot live and work there for weeks on end'.

Ministers went there once or twice afterwards but the worst of the bombing had ended as 1940 moved into 1941, and then Germany invaded Russia instead of England anyway. The forty armed guards were reduced to half a dozen. Paddock was abandoned at the end of 1944. Houses were built over it in late 1999, but Brent Council made Paddock a listed building and the developers were required to open it at least two days a year.

There's little to see now from the street. The surface building has been knocked down. The steel door of an emergency exit remains in a wall between houses. An access building altered to match the houses gives on to concrete steps to a steel door. Some of the original equipment remains, including the telephone exchange and a kitchen. The plant room for power and air conditioning is still there, with its machinery and fans. And the map room, the conference centre, remains, although empty of charts.

Paddock was for a yesterday that never came. Thankfully.

1942

THE CROOK WHO FOOLED HITLER

Nothing strikes you as unusual about Crespigny Road. It's just another 1920s suburban road of prosperous-looking detached homes, few of them alike. Those that don't have garages have cars parked where once their gardens had grass. The occasional tree softens the tone of anonymous commuter London. And yet No. 35 was different: it was a Secret Service safe house for spies who fooled Hitler.

Crespigny Road is east of the Edgware Road, between the M1 motorway and Hendon Way as it winds to the Brent Cross shopping centre. Why the Secret Service chose it is unclear. But in the war it housed agents including the debonair Eddie Chapman, known as Agent Zigzag.

MI5 makes no pretence about Agent Zizag, it says:

Eddie Chapman was a professional criminal in the years before the Second World War. He was a member of a 'jelly gang' which specialised in robbing safes by blowing them open using the explosive gelignite. His skill as a thief made him a good deal of money and allowed him to live the life of a wealthy playboy in Soho, mixing with the likes of Noel Coward, Ivor Novello and Marlene Dietrich.

It doesn't mention that Chapman joined the Coldstream Guards when he was 17, enjoying the uniform and pay and the fairly safe job of protecting the Tower of London but quickly growing tired of the discipline and restrictions. He profited from six days' leave after only nine months in the army and ran off with a girl he'd met in Soho. They lived on the run for two months before the army caught him, jailed him for eighty-four days and then threw him out with a dishonourable discharge. The way was open for a succession of petty jobs and then something better paid as a crook.

Living like that, and often on other people's money, was bound to attract the police. And sure enough, in February 1939 they found him in a restaurant in Jersey, where they wanted him for, among other things, burgling a nightclub. He fled, abandoning a puzzled girlfriend he never forgot, but eventually copped two years in jail with an extra year on top for trying to escape from prison.

Chapman was still locked up on the island when the Germans invaded. He didn't get out until October 1941. By then the Channel Islands were far less convivial. He was in a fix. He wanted to return to the mainland but clearly the Germans weren't going to let him. And on top of that, he was wanted there for other crimes. Still, better in unoccupied Britain than in occupied Jersey, and so he asked the Abwehr if it needed a spy.

The Abwehr may not have wanted a crook in its service but it wasn't getting much from the agents it believed it already had in Britain and it wasn't inclined to turn down a volunteer. And where there was one crook, there may be more: Chapman's friends back in London might just provide a network of informants more by the law. And, if like Chapman they were useful with explosives, they could become saboteurs.

The Germans took their chance and flew him to occupied France. There he trained for a year before being parachuted into the Fens on 16 December 1942, a better choice in mid-winter than the mountains of Wales or Scotland, which they had also considered. What they hadn't considered was that he would go straight to the police and turn himself in – an event that saved a step because decoders at Bletchley Park had picked up word that 'Fritzchen' was on his way.

Spymasters should never have conventional names, of course, and so Chapman was taken to an MI5 detention centre in west London called Camp 020. And there he was questioned by Tin Eye Stephens. Stephens – Lieutenant Colonel Robin Stephens – was a star interrogator who always wore a steel-rimmed monocle.

Chapman gave Tin Eye little resistance. He told of everything he had learned in France, about his spymasters there and what they expected of him in Britain. In fact, he was so free with his information that the British suspected for a long time that he was an unusually glib and clever plant. And, as gentlemen, they were troubled by Chapman's criminality and a habit of consorting with drunks and prostitutes to whom he might blab his story. Still, MI5 had turned all the other German agents it had found and it was sure that, even if Chapman wasn't all he seemed, it could turn him into a double agent as well. Tin Eye decided: 'Chapman should be used to the fullest extent … he genuinely means to work for the British against the Germans. By his courage and resourcefulness he is ideally fitted to be an agent.' He gave him the code name Zigzag and set him to work against his former employers.

It was then that he installed him at 35 Crespigny Road and instructed his police minders that not only should they not arrest him, they should save him from being arrested by anyone else, and that they should tactfully facilitate his visits to drinking dens and anywhere else he sought company.

The Germans had wanted Chapman because he knew about explosives. They taught him still more while they had him at their spy school. And now they told him to blow up the factory in Hatfield, north of London, that built Mosquito bombers. The Mosquito was a particular nuisance because, with its wooden frame and without the weight of guns, it could fly faster than any of the fighters sent to intercept reconnaissance flights.

Chapman did indeed blow up the factory, on the night of 29 January 1943. Or, rather, with MI5's connivance, he produced a loud bang and what from reconnaissance planes would look like a convincing amount of damage. The factory was untouched but looked wrecked thanks to overnight camouflage devised by theatrical designers and supervised by MI5. If Germany could be persuaded that Chapman had blown the place apart then the Luftwaffe could be sent elsewhere and Hatfield could get on building its wooden wonders.

Chapman boasted of his success to the Germans and the *Daily Express* swallowed its principles and reported the factory's end, knowing it would be read in Germany. Berlin was so thrilled that it awarded Chapman the Iron Cross during a spying visit to Norway. He is the only Briton ever to have held it.

Britain and Germany then sent him to Portugal, from where Berlin told him to return to London to report on the effectiveness of its V1 flying bombs. He parachuted back into the Fens and, using an established Morse code signal to show that he was free of the British, falsely reported that the bombs were passing over their target. The Germans therefore shortened their range so that they fell not in central London but in the southern suburbs.

By now the Secret Service was growing unhappy with what else was going on in Chapman's life. Tin Eye may have seen the benefits outweighing the embarrassing aspects but a later handler was distinctly hostile. And well he might have been, because Chapman had taken to doping greyhounds to make a killing on betting. He had also started blabbing, and so on 2 November 1944 his spymasters gave him £6,000 and £1,000 of the money the Germans had given him, arranged a pardon for his crimes, and told him to go away.

If they hoped he'd vanish, they were disappointed. He involved himself in blackmail and theft and with smuggling gold. Legend says that MI5 stepped in at least once to give him a character reference and arrange for charges to be dropped. He was convicted under the Official Secrets Act for publishing his story in France. The *News of the World* printed the story and had to pulp an entire issue.

He did, though, set up a health retreat at Shenley, north of London. He stayed friendly with his German handler and helped him when he fell on hard times, and after a complicated love life he found and married the woman, Betty Farmer, from whom he'd fled in the Hôtel des Plages in Jersey when the police rushed in.

He died in December 1997, of heart failure.

Did anyone in Crespigny Road know what was going on there? Some may have wondered, of course. A succession of seemingly unattached men, some of them authoritative, all of them secretive, wouldn't have gone unnoticed. But the culture was not to say, not to ask.

The Secret Service released their grip on No. 35 and it went back to being a private house. It's changed over the years but its past is no longer secret. There's a blue plaque on the wall but, to the end, it denies Eddie Chapman. It records instead the residency of a later agent, the Spaniard Juan Pujol Garcia, even though he and his wife later moved to nearby Elliot Road.

Both men deceived the Germans. Chapman was the more daring but he was also the more criminal. Garcia – Agent Garbo – had the more obvious effect on the war, however, not only running a network of German spies in Britain who had never existed and for which the Germans paid, but sending these agents' supposed messages in a way that misled Berlin about the invasion of Normandy.

1943

DAMBUSTER IN CHIEF

Beyond Edgware Road Tube station, the road itself crosses a canal. To the left, tour boats putter up and down from an area fancifully known as Little Venice. They plunge into darkness as they reach the Edgware Road and carry on that way the length of the Maida Hill tunnel. On the surface runs Aberdeen Place. And 32 Aberdeen Place is where Guy Gibson used to live. There's a plaque on the wall to say so.

Guy Gibson was once better known, not least in 1954 when a film, *The Dam Busters*, celebrated the raid that he led to drop water-skipping bombs on dams in wartime Germany. His 617 Squadron was based at RAF Scampton, north of Lincoln (it's now at Marham, in Norfolk). It was at Aberdeen Place that he lived with his wife, Eve, when he was off duty.

The RAF celebrates him now but originally it turned him down because he wasn't tall enough. He was 5ft 6in, with disproportionately short legs. Once accepted, he made fast progress. He became a wing commander in April 1942, taking charge of 106 Squadron as it moved to the new Lancaster bombers. Arthur Harris, nicknamed Bomber Harris, believed that only heavy bombing could ruin German war production and, extended to civilian targets and entire cities, demoralise the population into surrender. That was the Lancaster's purpose.

In reality, neither happened – industrial destruction or public despair, that is – and the dam-busting raid was a sign of that. That, however, is not to take away from the brilliance of its conception and execution. The objective was to demolish six dams that held back reservoirs that helped power Germany's industrial heartland in the Ruhr Valley. Not only would the hydro-electric plants be destroyed but the valley would be flooded and its factories with it.

The problem was that the dams were in tight valleys. If – and it was a big if – they could be bombed conventionally, there was little chance that the explosions would damage them and every chance that the bombers would be shot down. The solution came from an engineer and inventor called Barnes Wallis, who had by then designed the Wellington bomber. Wallis concluded that the only way to destroy the dams was to drop the bombs some distance back from the dams and make them skip along the water like a stone until they reached them. They would then roll down the wall and explode closer to its foundations. To do that, Lancasters would have to fly at just 18m. To put that in perspective, Nelson's column is 52m.

Gibson led the raid on the night of 16 May 1943. It had spectacular propaganda success and passed into British legend but it achieved much less than the strategists hoped. Just two of the dams – the Möhne and Eder – were damaged enough to destroy the power generators and flood the valleys. The price was the death of 1,600 civilians, most of them women, most of them French, Belgian, Polish or Soviet prisoners of war or forced labourers. The Germans shot down eight Lancasters and killed fifty-three of the crew, two of every five. Gibson was awarded the Victoria Cross, the highest of British medals. He had not only led the raid but flown beside the other bombers to distract the German gunners.

He was not a popular man. The English Heritage webpage on Gibson's blue plaque stated that 'Gibson was always eager to fly on operations, trying to prove himself. His conduct sometimes verged on the arrogant, attracting nicknames of "Bumptious Bastard" and "The Boy Emperor".' Another history remembers that he often flew into a public temper with his ground crew and once came close to demoting a corporal who didn't salute him. By others he was said to be hard-working, efficient, straightforward and sociable.

Eve was at 32 Aberdeen Place when a telegram arrived to say he was dead. He is buried in the town of Steenbergen – 'stone hills' – in south-west Holland. He and his co-pilot crashed there in a Mosquito bomber on the night of 19 September 1944. His white gravestone is in the style common to Commonwealth graveyards. It reads: 'Wing Commander G.P. Gibson VC, DSO and bar, DFC and bar, pilot, Royal Air Force, 19th September 1944, age 26.' Above the inscription is the symbol of the Royal Air Force and, beneath it, a representation of his Victoria Cross and its legend, 'For Valour'.

The story of the raid was unknown in America when the film was shown there with Richard Todd playing Gibson. So many disbelieved it that it was withdrawn and an opening caption added to explain that the events portrayed were true.

Gibson did not devise or plan the dam raids, but the fact that they happened led to such raids being declared a war crime.

1944

BRITISH TOMMY HELPS WIN THE WAR

When Tommy Flowers was getting on a bit, his family gave him a laptop computer. It interested him but he wasn't sure how to use it. So he enrolled for an evening class, a long-faced man with white hair and tired eyes but a ready smile. He sat there among the teenage would-be programmers and took in what the teacher told him. Nobody knew who he was. And then one of the younger men saw his name on the list of students.

He hesitated. And then, respectfully, he went to the old man and asked: 'You wouldn't be *the* Thomas Flowers?'

And Tommy Flowers smiled and agreed that, yes, he was. He had invented the world's first programmable electronic computer. Back then, in the 1940s, a single computer filled a whole room and had thousands of glowing valves. Now here he was with a gadget the size of a folded newspaper that had more computing power than anything he had invented to help Bletchley Park solve the thousands of German coded messages that arrived there each week.

The secret decoding centre at first broke messages by pencil and brainpower. It then built a machine to automate part of the job. It was a partly mechanical, partly electronic device. It worked, it helped, but it was slow and unreliable.

Tommy Flowers worked at the Dollis Hill Post Office laboratories, the ones that had the government war centre tunnelled beneath them. Few people knew more about practical electronics than he did. He told the code-breakers in February 1943 that he could make them a Thinking Machine. And they scoffed, not only because it sounded ridiculous but because it would need 1,600 thermionic valves and only one would have to fail for the whole thing to stop and lose the information it held.

Flowers retorted that new valves were reliable. They failed if they were turned on and off too much, he agreed, so he said don't turn them off. Bletchley Park listened but still said no. Flowers went home disillusioned but not deterred. The Post Office knew his work better than civil servants did, and he persuaded Dollis Hill to let him work on his machine largely in his own time and out of his own pocket. He finished his Colossus in ten months.

It would be good to think that Bletchley Park blushed and apologised when the new computer hummed into activity in January 1944. It could work out German codes in hours and not weeks. It was followed six months later by a still more powerful version that took 2,400 valves. There were ten by the end of the war. With peace, though, any mention of it was forbidden by secrecy laws. Eight of the computers were taken to bits and two were sent to London. Whether they were used or stored is unclear, that being part of the secret. Churchill was worried that the Russians would learn of them; a cold war was on the way. If the computers could be built once, he reasoned, they could be built again.

Not until the 1970s was it acknowledged that Colossus had existed. Before that, Tommy Flowers had gone from bank to bank for a loan to build more Thinking Machines. Managers waved him away as a fanciful dreamer, while, because of secrecy laws, Flowers couldn't say that not only did such things once exist but that he had created them.

Flowers saw the world catch up with him but with the twist that he no longer recognised the offspring of his creation, let alone know how to use them. Which is how he came to be at the evening class where he was nervously asked if he was *the* Thomas Flowers.

He died in 1998. The Post Office labs at Dollis Hill, by then part of British Telecom, closed in 1975 and moved to Martlesham in Suffolk. A street is named after him where the Dollis Hill labs once were. A grateful nation paid him £1,000, a fraction of his own money that he had spent, and he divided it with those he worked with. He was made an MBE, the lowest of the three ranks (commander, order and member) and the one given to long-serving postmistresses and lollipop ladies.

Decades later, Bill Clinton told the world that America had invented the computer.

1944

SEX AND SMUT

The Paddington Estate lies beside the Edgware Road just south of where it's now crossed by Westway. The prostitution conducted enthusiastically there in the 1940s brought clients from across London. And the best of it is that the area was owned not by vice kings but by the Church of England. It had been in religious hands since 959.

The busiest area was near Paddington station, where cheap hotels neighboured each other along Praed Street, Sussex Gardens and Norfolk Square. In November 1944 the *Paddington Mercury* held no punches:

> The Church knows that it is one of the worst districts in London for prostitution. It knows that a large proportion of the £84,000 rent income helps to pay the stipends of its clergy. But it has no legal power to interfere with the traffic. And it does not regard the money so received as 'tainted' for it is received not from brothel keepers but from perfectly respectable people.

The estate stretched across 600 acres north of Bayswater Road and west of the Edgware Road. It was lively enough before the Second World War but, come 1939, thousands on leave and away from home took the train into London and then to the Church's estate. A doctor writing in *The Times* on 5 August 1942 reported that venereal disease had become 20 per cent worse because of what he called the 'white slave trade' there. Paddington and Euston were the worst places, he said.

It put the Church into a fluster. In the absence of a plan, it created a committee almost a year later. It took a further nine months to suggest that bishops should raise the topic in the House of Lords. That angered *The Mercury*. The Church was more interested in showing its innocence than doing anything about what was happening in houses from which it was taking a rent, it accused.

The law outlawed solicitation on the street and a 'common prostitute' could be fined. But working indoors brought a legal loophole. Brothels were illegal but the definition of a brothel was that a room had to be used by more than one woman. There was no offence if prostitutes rented their own room. The Church said it was powerless to control them. *The Mercury* set out to show that it wasn't. It reported tenants under a law on the more general suppression of brothels. That made it possible to fine the landlord or tenant or send him to jail for up to three months. The paper gleefully published the cases it covered at Marylebone police court.

The police typically watched a building for three or four days or nights. They counted the numbers entering. Often they knew which women were prostitutes. If the numbers worked out, they raided. Courts fined small-scale operators £10 if they confessed, adding on the court's costs. Old lags who insisted they were innocent could be jailed for three months. The paper reported on a 65-year-old woman twice sent to jail for three months. Another woman was fined £30 and her Italian husband was jailed for a month.

Of one house, the police said there were girls there with American, Canadian and British servicemen. The men were picked up on the street and brought to hotels known not to fuss about identities, marriage certificates or even how long a room was rented. So-called 'good-time girls' – many found the word 'prostitute' socially difficult – 'threw themselves' especially on Americans, known to have more money and to be further from home.

The women were so numerous and so blatant that they became known as Piccadilly Commandos. They charged £5 for a quickie or £25 for longer. An American airman remembered the newspaper seller on the pavement there shouting 'Paper! Paper!' before adding, more quietly, 'Condoms, condoms!' A poster showing an American sailor stepping out with his kitbag on his shoulder asked: 'Taking VD home, too, sailor?'

Most hotels had long-term residents but the hotels' owners usually explained that times were as hard for their business as everyone else and they had the cost of keeping their hotel open. Some buildings, though, were not hotels. Landlords rented rooms to whoever would pay, prostitutes or not. Scotland Yard said there were sixty women in one building, paying £5 a week for up to twenty customers a day. A soldier found with a girl told police he had come indoors to sit by the fire.

The girls were fined. The men were fined. The one group that was never prosecuted was the Ecclesiastical Commissioners. They carried on collecting their rents.

1950

THE ARAB CONNECTION

Walk along the London end of the Edgware Road and the signs outside many shops and cafés may be written in gorgeous curving script. And from right to left. It's Arabic. Those who write it are often Muslim, and from the Gulf, fewer from northern Africa.

Nobody knows for sure why to be south of the Marylebone flyover should have been attractive to Arabic-speaking immigrants. Wars are a pretty good guess. Much of the Arab world is a troubled world. Thousands fled from the Ottoman Empire's brutality. Its rulers held supreme over everywhere east of Italy. The empire's decline was assured only in the drawing of boundaries at the end of the First World War and sealed when Turkey became independent in 1923.

Many of those who fled there and elsewhere were attracted to London because of its international reputation, because English is many people's second language, and because of Britain's colonial links with the Near East. Britain, after all, has variously ruled and even created states in the region.

Accounts agree that London has long appealed to Egyptians, Palestinians (later arrivals having been displaced by border disputes with and attacks by Israel), Lebanese and others. Immigrants from all regions go first to areas where housing is inexpensive and where they will meet people from home. Not all Arab immigrants are fabulously wealthy.

Immigrant populations often move on, and some Arabs in London have indeed dispersed to more distant suburbs. But now and then, like the world's various Chinatowns, they make a district their own. That distinctiveness then attracts tourists as well as further immigrants. And so it seems to have been in the Edgware Road.

Gulf News quotes the BBC as saying that half a million Arabs live in the UK. Professional or unskilled, they came to work, most from Egypt and Morocco. 'Some also arrived from the Gulf to set up businesses in the UK,' says *Gulf News*.

'And the Lebanese flocked there after the civil war, as did the Iraqis and others from Arab countries.'

It continues:

It is common to see them in the jellabiah (an Arabic robe) with their heads covered in the traditional ghutra (white Arabic head dress). Despite the cosmopolitan nature of London, Arabs have not integrated into European society, but have retained their way of life. They still look odd in this community. On Edgware Road, the Lebanese have taken advantage of the growth of London's café society, opening up coffee shops and patisseries all over the area.

1951

TO WORK 'TIL YOU'RE DEAD
FOR A ROOM AND A BED

There's a song about the Irish in 1950s Britain that's hard to find these days. It tells of the sad life of poor country boys who came to London to send some money home, but ended up instead broken and sometimes alcoholic and certainly no better than they had been before. The reality of their dreams was to be employed by the day, to drink in the evening and to sleep in a crowded hostel by night. The touching line in the song summed it up: to work 'til you're dead for a room and a bed.

Britain used to send troops and governors abroad; Ireland sent its people. It sent so many that the population fell from 8.2 million in 1841 to 4.2 million in 1961. Most who left went to America, where more people claim to be Irish than ever lived on the island. Political changes intervened from 1920 and emigrants went not west but east, to Britain.

Two things coincided. The first is that Ireland had long had larger families than agricultural communities could support. One academic explained that a family with six sons had more labour than it needed on the farm but, of those, only one would inherit the land. The other five faced spending their lives as labourers with bed and board and just enough money to get by. America had offered possibilities, but later it was less keen and the attraction was to go to Britain, where buildings had to be torn down and replaced, roads laid, new houses built. Those who came from Kerry and the other impoverished counties may have known little of laying bricks but they knew about digging. And dig they did.

Nobody knows how many left. There are no exit figures and none for Irishmen arriving in Britain, where they have had passport-free access since the days when Ireland was part of the United Kingdom. A figure of half a million seems a reasonable estimate for the 1950s alone. And many stood beside the roads leading out of London, often with shovels on their shoulders, waiting for contractors' vans to stop if they were needed. If they weren't, they returned home without pay for the day. They became known and celebrated as McAlpine's Fusiliers, after one of the largest building contractors of the period and whose half-vans, half-buses were a familiar sight.

So many Irishmen settled in Kilburn that, moving the syllabic stress to the end, the area became known as Co. Kil*burn*. Why there? Because it was cheap.

Kilburn and nearby Camden Town had always been a poor area. There were houses along the Edgware Road by the 1850s but grander accommodation had never succeeded. Kilburn remained deprived. The poor were there and more arrived. Kilburn is part of Willesden and Willesden's population more than quadrupled in ten years, from 3,879 in 1861 to 15,869 in 1871. Most of that was in Kilburn. By 1890, one family in five in Kilburn was living in poverty, and that by a scale far more severe than we know today. South Kilburn in 1954 had an average of ten people to a house.

For those who came to work, there was a hostel if the price of a room elsewhere was too great. Arlington House was once the largest hostel in Europe. It packed in 1,200 homeless men, mostly Irish immigrants. Lord Rowton – Montagu Lowry-Corry – opened it in 1905, that and five others, as a philanthropic gesture to the poor.

The building, which is still there, was the closest to home that men fresh from the train south from the Dun Laoghaire ferry could find. The writer Peter Kavanagh spent time there. He said 'the soft voices of Mayo and Galway … in that gaunt impersonal place fell like warm rain on the arid patches of my imagination'. Even so, there were just six baths for 180 men, many of whom returned grubby from the ditches they had dug. There were, still are, six storeys. A metal staircase turns in loops between institutional white-tiled walls.

The men's problem was the very simplicity of the lives they had led before, a farm life in which money counted for little, because there wasn't much, and where taxes weren't a consideration because wages were a share of what was grown and eaten. They came unskilled and often not literate. They spoke with accents that the British found hard to understand and, in the way of London and other populations, they were rejected. 'No dogs, no Irish' was a common sign in lodging house windows, sometimes topped by 'No blacks'.

It meant the Irish fell back within themselves. A grapevine explained how to find a job or, better put, how to find work. Stand on this corner or that corner at dawn, shovel on shoulder, and wait for a contractor to pass. If men were needed, the van would halt. If five men were needed that day, five men got in. The rest waited for another van, if there was one, or went home without pay.

One recalled: 'Before I ever left home, I knew all you had to do was go to Camden Town and you'd get work: just pick a colour – RSK was brown, Murphy green or grey, Lowry was blue, Pincher Mac was green.'

The men rarely knew where they were going. Labouring on one site was pretty much like labouring on another. Dig here, mix cement there. Wages came in cash, often with some skimmed off the top by the foreman and always after the gangmaster had deducted from what the developer had paid.

There was 'good money on the buildings, but no insurance stamp, and no sick pay if you got hurt, or dole if you were out of work. Getting paid in pubs and having to buy the foreman drinks. Getting a "sub" on Wednesday to get through to Friday, assuming you were working.'

'There was a high status to it because of the high wages,' said another immigrant worker, 'or what we considered high wages at the time. People were proud that they were working class and getting good money for it.'

But it was hard, and if you couldn't do it, others would. 'If you were diggin' out a road,' one boss remembered, 'you'd mark off every 35 yards with a piece of chalk, and tell a new man: "If you can't finish that before this evenin', don't come in tomorrow. You get paid for the shit you shift."'

They were known as navvies, because earlier Irishmen came to dig out the canals to create the Inland Navigation System. The Irish then weren't the majority; they joined men recruited on the spot. And they were already resented as outsiders. North of London, the Irish helped dig the way for the London–Birmingham railway line as it passed through the Chilterns at Tring. The local paper reported on 30 September 1836:

> There was a great riot here today. A party of Irish navvies passing through the town were attacked by parties of navvies working on the L&B railroad. The Irish navvies were knocked down, severely beaten, stones thrown at them, and dogs were set on them to tear them. The Irishmen returned again later in the day, and there was a great riot in the town. Several inhabitants of the town assembled and took some of the rioters into custody. There has been a lot of disturbances in the neighbourhood with these men, many of whom are but rough uncouth savages, as fierce as tigers.

They did other things as well, of course, and always had. Irish street traders had sold nuts and oranges since the 1820s. Jack Black, dressed in jacket, breeches and soft top hat, called himself 'rat and mole destroyer to Her Majesty'. He sold domesticated rats to 'well-bred young ladies to keep in squirrel cages'.

These early 'street Irish' spoke Gaelic, sometimes a little English, their wives no English at all. A hundred thousand had arrived in London by 1851. Most were illiterate.

And so it remained as Britain sought workers after 1945 to replace its war dead – Ireland had been neutral – and to build new roads and suburbs. The problem, said Clement Attlee, the post-war prime minister, wasn't that there was too little work; it was that there were too few people to do it. That was exaggerated by Britain's conscripting young people for military service.

London Transport advertised for single men of 19 or more and women older than 20 to become bus drivers and conductors. 'Selected applicants will have their fares paid to London,' the advertisements said. The National Health Service called for trainee nurses. Work was easy to find; visit a labour exchange in the morning and you'd have a job by the afternoon, one worker remembered.

More than that, the Edgware Road had small factories that are no longer there. Times were hard after the war, but work needed to be done, men needed to be employed. Those with skills, it was said, could walk along the Edgware Road one morning and have a job in a factory for the next morning.

Life was different for the unskilled. Many men spoke of their life's hardships, how they were locked into a succession of pouring concrete or pulling down walls. At the end of each day and the end of each week, they had just their small room. The only light was often recalled as the company of other Irishmen down at the pub, complaining, perhaps, but revelling in their Irishness.

Getting out of a dreary room and to the pub was the limit of many labourers' lives. 'You couldn't just walk the street,' one said. 'What could you do? You'd end up going to the pub just to talk to someone.' For many, already poorly paid, well rewarded for labouring but far from wealthy, and exploited by those who employed them, the pub was all there was. And pubs could be rough. Bernard Canavan remembers: 'The pub was an employment agency, a place to change cheques, an eating house, it was everything. It was a very macho world. There were lots of fights which were quite violent and the image men wanted was of being tough. There were places I would not have come in at that time. You would see people spewing out into the streets and people were beaten.'

Another memory, published by *The Irish Times* as part of the opinion series 'An Irishman's Diary', 11 June 2004:

> The Crown in Cricklewood [was] a big seething barn of drink and noise and smoke ... It was not for the faint-hearted. Brendan Bowyer, Bridie Gallagher and Larry Cunningham on a permanent loop on the jukebox, a ceilidh band in a corner. The aftermath of a fist fight, the danger of being "glassed" by someone who didn't like the way you were looking at him – or the county you came from ... There were glasses flyin' and Biddies cryin' and the Paddies were going to town.

Some of Kilburn's Irish prospered, moved out and up the social ladder. There aren't many Irish voices in town these days. Only 5 per cent of Kilburn's population is now Irish and most of those are older people who've stayed. The others have been replaced by later immigrants, especially from the Caribbean. Some Irish, though, were too beaten, in the pubs or by their labour in all weather. Some became alcoholics. A few made enough money to send home, or to return home themselves. But many more spent their money within a few hundred yards of where they were paid it. And never having paid tax or health contributions, they fell ill or simply died young.

But for many years yet, Kilburn will be associated with short men, difficult accents, old jackets and folded-down wellingtons. They joked that: 'We'll give back Kilburn if the Brits give us back the north of Ireland.'

Dominic Behan's song 'McAlpine's Fusiliers' remembers men like that, how they 'sweated blood and washed down mud, with pints and quarts of beer'.

They worked 'til they were dead, for a room and a bed.

1956

JACK SPOT, PROFESSIONAL GANGSTER

Mad Frankie Fraser wasn't called that for nothing. He said he would have been happy to butcher Jack 'Spot' Comer for nothing because cutting up a rival gangster would seal his reputation on the streets. Being paid as well was a bonus.

They made a good pair, Fraser and Comer. Although 'good' is perhaps not the right word. Fraser was a member of the Richardson Gang in the 1960s. The Richardsons controlled London south of the river, the Kray twins the north. Each resented any trespass on their territory.

As is often the case, the war between them began not because of a major transgression but because one of the Richardson gang, George Cornell, called Ronnie Kray a 'fat poof' during a Christmas party in December 1965. Truth often hurts and Kray was sensitive on both counts. Cornell paid for his indiscretion by being shot dead in the Blind Beggar pub in the East End.

Members of both gangs were terrifying and it didn't pay to speak against them. When Fraser was tried for murder, a witness changed his testimony and the case was dropped. The Richardsons tortured those they decided were disloyal. Fraser obliged by pulling out the teeth of their victims with pliers. He was jailed for ten years for that, among the forty-two he spent in more than twenty prisons.

But there was a pecking order. Even the Kray twins looked up to Jack 'Spot' Comer, or Jacob Colmore as he had been born, an older thug who had been fighting since his earliest days. Comer's father, a tailor, had fled anti-Jewish pogroms in Łódź, Poland, in around 1900. He changed his name from Comacho to Colmore and then to Comer. They lived in Fieldgate Mansions in Whitechapel.

Comer junior was born on 12 April 1912. He joined his first gang at 7, siding with Jewish boys in the East End who fought Catholics from the other end of the street, and was soon a good brawler. He moved up the scale in violence and claimed to have attacked the fascist leader, Oswald Mosley, and his bodyguards in a battle in Cable Street (a claim that has been much disputed, it has to be said). Comer said he was called Spot because he was always on the spot when there was trouble, especially against fellow Jews. Others say it was because of a mole on his cheek and that Comer glamourised his nickname.

Comer said that East End Jews were easy victims, that their customers would walk away with suits they refused to pay for or from bookmakers whom they refused to refund what they owed. He stood outside their shops, he said, 'and when I was there, they paid for everything'.

He and his gangs took over nightclubs in Leeds and Birmingham, then moved on to racecourses. Detective Sergeant Mickey Downe said in a film of Comer's life:

> Spot relied indeed on muscle and, of course, the menace, which was of course the grimace and the half sneer on his face. Which in any sort of dim light could be very, very frightening and you could well understand that someone running a café or a restaurant or anything else, when confronted by this man, who loomed closer and closer to you, his face shaking and his eyes in slits, would indeed be very, very frightening.

Comer moved into the West End after the war, running illegal drinking and gaming clubs and demanding protection money from competitors. He carried razors he acquired from his brother, a barber. London had never seen such organised crime.

Nipper Read, who put the Krays behind bars – he got his nickname as a fast-moving youthful boxer – said:

> Jack Spot epitomised all that there was about the old-time, Mafia-style gangster. He was always immaculately dressed. He always looked the part. He would come out of his flat every morning and go over to the station and go to the barber's and sit in the chair while they did his hair and gave him a shave and so on. And then in his brown suit and a brown overcoat and a brown fedora hat, he would march down Edgware Road and receive the accolades.

Comer operated not alone but through gangs he recruited for specific jobs. He corrupted policemen and MPs to smooth his way. But crime was a jealous world and he fell out with a colleague, and with an Italian rival, who set out to depose him. They wrecked his bars and gambling venues. They waited for days outside one of his gambling clubs, waiting to attack him, then lost interest and attacked him and his 27-year-old wife, Margaret, known as Rita, outside their house in Hyde Park Mansions, Cabbell Street, instead. It's just off the Edgware Road, in Marylebone, opposite Edgware Road station.

Frankie Fraser and other masked thugs butchered him and then cut off his left ear. It took 300 stitches to close the wounds and sew back the ear, which Comer had picked up and put in his pocket. The attack made the main headline on the front page of papers including the *Daily Express*, so widely known had Comer become.

Comer declined to give evidence at the trial. Fraser went back to prison for seven years, joined by his gang, despite his lawyer describing him as a 'weaker vessel of mankind who has been used for a foul purpose'. Fraser was also certified insane.

Comer, surprisingly, survived but he slowly dropped out of crime, selling antiques, working as a greengrocer in Isleworth, and attending boxing matches. He was declared bankrupt in 1959 and died in Isleworth on 12 March 1996. He was 84, penniless and without his wife and children. His ashes were scattered in Israel.

1958

GREEN LICKING

There was a time when grocers' shops were run by a man dressed in brown. He stood behind a cluttered counter and reached into his shelves for your packet of tea or, in those days before decimals, 2lb of sugar. In quieter shops, a cat might doze in the window.

Whether you shopped there or anywhere else made no difference. Your tube of toothpaste or box of soap powder cost just the same everywhere else. The company that made or imported what you wanted told the shopkeeper what to charge for it. And refused to supply him with that or anything else if he set a price of his own.

It was called retail price maintenance. Companies insisted that it worked in the interests of customers because it kept small shops open and convenient. It seemed normal at the time. More than 44 per cent of what 1950s customers spent was controlled by these rigid prices.

But there are ways round many rules. Richard Tompkins – his first name was Granville but he never used it – was born in Islington, north London, in 1918. It was a month after the end of the First World War. Few people expected him to do much in life. He worked in a laundry, he worked on a petrol station forecourt in the days before drivers filled their cars themselves, and he ran a small café. There was no sign he would make millions, though he did open a printing business.

He was 40 when he went to Chicago. It was there that he saw shops hand green stamps to customers with their change. They were called simply Green Stamps. They were handed over in proportion to the money spent, they could be saved and then cashed for goods from a catalogue. Tompkins returned to Britain and saw that Fine Fare, a supermarket chain, had already started giving stamps, but American S&H stamps from Sperry and Hutchinson.

Why did they give them? Because while shops could not undercut the obligatory prices, they could give back cash in the form of stamps. And that circumvented retail price maintenance.

Tompkins saw his chance and quickly set up his own company. He called it Green Shield, copying Green Stamps in the USA. That was 1958, the year he went to America. The business grew and in the early 1960s Tompkins opened a white and unattractive square office block in Station Road, Edgware, several steps back from the Edgware Road. He called it Premier House.

From most of its dozen floors the view was over the coal yard at the failed Edgware railway station. Not the Tube station down the road; that came later. The steam station, opened by the Great Northern, failed in a muddle. It had fourteen trains a day at its peak, running in a curve that led to the terminus at King's Cross. London Transport planned to electrify the line and then extend it over the Northern Heights, a plan to extend the Northern Line out to Bushey Heath, now part of Watford. It was cancelled by the Second World War and later planning regulations.

By then the steam line was neither one thing nor another. Freight trains continued until 1964 and the coal businesses it supplied were easily visible from Green Shield's Premier House. From Premier House, the company sold stamps to retailers, and retailers gave them in ever-increasing quantities to customers. Garages in particular boasted of double, triple and even quadruple stamps. More than 36,000 companies signed up, each having to compete with or outbid its competitors, petrol stations having to draw off passing trade. Some drivers would press on with their fuel gauge showing empty, just for the chance of a better deal on stamps.

Green Shield became hugely profitable as a result. It was, after all, neither making nor distributing anything other than sheets of gummed paper.

Tompkins was a square-faced man with thick-framed glasses. He was said at one time to be Britain's most highly paid executive. But within a few years of moving to the top floor of his rectangular office block, he could see that price maintenance was already collapsing under its own weight. The first supermarkets were just ignoring it, challenging suppliers to cut them off.

It was John Stonehouse who brought about the end. Stonehouse is better remembered now, if he is remembered at all, as the Labour MP who faked his death in 1974 to escape the private scandals that were embracing him. Retail price maintenance and trading stamps had already been a political divide. Conservatives were torn between the progressives, like Edward Heath at the Board of Trade, and the traditionalists who wanted to do nothing to harm, as they saw it, the profits of businessmen who supported them.

In the end, it was the Labour MP, Stonehouse, who proposed a Private Members Bill to outlaw trading stamps. Conservatives were obliged to support or to challenge him. Heath both supported him and went further. As his biographer, John Campbell, says: 'He was determined to put his name to some major piece of legislation before the election. If it had to be the abolition of RPM, so be it … If it was a challenge that previous ministers had ducked, so much the better for his "tough" image.'

By then, Tompkins had seen how things were changing. If trading stamps were to be no more, perhaps customers would part with cash instead. If the price was right. So he opened a chain of shops named Argos, a name he chose partly because it would be high in alphabetical lists. He was pushed gently into it when Tesco, one of his first customers for stamps, dropped him and lowered its prices instead.

Argos opened many branches but it never had the immediate something-for-nothing appeal of stamps. The company changed hands several times, owned for a period by Anglo-American, the cigarette maker.

Tompkins developed cancer. He died in central London in 1992, the year he was made a CBE and a year after his stamp empire came to an end. He was 72. He gave much of his fortune away. He set up his own charity, the Tompkins Foundation, in 1980, to dispose of it. The foundation continues to this day, its motive remaining Tompkins' original wish, that it support 'the advancement of education and learning, religion, the provision of facilities for recreation and other purposes beneficial to the community.'

Premier House still stands in Station Road, Edgware. It is now a block of flats, redecorated on the outside to disguise its matchbox bleakness.

1960

WATER SPORTS

The people who organised the post-war Olympics in London in 1948 were convinced they'd done a good job despite the shortages and wrecked venues.

They were so convinced that they produced an account of the organisation to help those who followed. It's so comprehensive that it's 4cm thick, with the dimensions of an old-fashioned schoolboys' and girls' annual. In it, you read that the Olympic flame was turned down at night to save gas but had to be put back on full blast a few days later when word spread that it had gone out. You find too that teams landing at airports all over the place overcame the transport managers and that they decided to meet only British airlines. You find that the running track at Wembley was made of the chimney sweepings of houses in Leicester, and that wild-spirited cyclists commandeered one of the buses and took it to Windsor and their road-race course, driving it around until they were relieved of the keys.

It also says that the rowing races were at Henley, where the annual regatta provided most of the facilities. What it doesn't say is that they were organised on the Welsh Harp. Which is a pity, because legend says, wrongly, that they were. That's confusion, perhaps, with the European championships for women in 1960 that were indeed on the reservoir. They had been run since 1954, when they were in Amsterdam. London simply took over the borough regatta that had been run for years.

The same Olympic frugality applied, though: the female competitors were sent not to hotels nor even a temporary village but to John Kelly Girls School, further up Dollis Hill from the equally down-to-earth Neasden recreation ground.

The rowers started arriving on 7 August. They installed themselves in dormitories in classrooms equipped with 'hard as board' mattresses from the War Department. It was an odd place to hold an opening party. A party with much linguistic confusion, too, because teams came from Belgium, Romania (still spelled Roumania in reports of the races), Yugoslavia (spelled Jugoslavia in the local style), USSR, Czechoslovakia, Austria, Hungary, Poland, Germany (a last-moment concoction because the international association did not recognise East Germany; in the end both countries competed as Germany, each in its own colours, each in its own boat), Holland, Greece, France and Norway, as well as a home team.

The championships would start with a 'grand display of fireworks', said the poster. There would be entertainment by the bands of the Coldstream Guards and the Scots Guards, an amusement park with 'Holland's gigantic funfair – all the latest rides and amusements', and a licensed buffet. The Duke of Edinburgh was in charge of the opening. Tickets cost 2s.

'Deep Slavonic roars of encouragement echoed across the grey waters of the Welsh Harp as the strong-limbed ladies of Europe swept their fragile craft towards the finishing line,' reported one local paper. And the water was indeed grey; as grey as everything else because the weather was cloudy and windy and the crowd of 5,000 was fewer than the organisers hoped. Those who stayed at home could watch some of the events on television.

They were disappointed if they hoped for local domination: Eastern Europe trounced the rest, with the USSR winning the eights, coxed fours and double sculls, and Hungary taking the single sculls. Germany won the quadruple sculls. Britain reached two finals and came last in both.

There were no men's championships because 1960 was Olympics year and the men went to Rome instead. Women's rowing did not become an Olympic sport until 1976, in Montreal. Had the men raced, the events would not have been in north London. Their rules specified a 2,000m course, the women's half that distance. It was only just possible to fit a 1,000m course within the Welsh Harp so that the events could take place. Even then, they started hard against the bank. One competitor, Penny Chuter of Britain, remembered: 'To get 1,000 metres in, on the first stroke your blades were literally in waterweed – horrible green slimy stuff.'

Willesden Council put up much of the cost and the Amateur Rowing Association a further £290 12s 8d, which seems to have been spent on hospitality for international delegates. The pace boat supplied by Regent Street Polytechnic's men's team to draw out the eight-woman team in training hit a submerged milk crate and sank. Alsatians guarded the championship boats at night. The British team had to sew on their Union Jacks and each letter of the country's name. They also had to pay for their clothing: £3 for the tracksuit, £4 15s for a blazer, and 12s 6d for a shirt. They were allowed to pay in instalments. The British got on best with the Romanians because they shared French as a second language, and a taste for whisky.

The Dutch carried their boats to the water while wearing clogs. The British felt like orphans in their shapeless kit when they stood beside the tailored foreign teams. The Russians were seen taking copious tablets, supposedly vitamin pills, which they offered to share. 'They were all on it,' one British rower remembered. 'We were more streetwise than they were, poor dears. They really thought that they *were* vitamin pills.'

1970

CONCRETE DEFEAT

Someone has painted trees on the discoloured concrete supports. The road they hold up at only twice head height is so wide that the sun never shines on some of the pavement beneath. Six hundred buildings were knocked down and an estimated 3,356 people had to be rehoused to make a journey of 2½ miles two minutes faster. Houses beside the road were bought against their owners' will, rented to whoever would have them for a few weeks at a time, or left derelict.

Westway is 2½ miles of road from the flyover that takes traffic over the Edgware Road. It passes Paddington Green and ends shortly afterwards. It opened on 28 July 1970 despite years of protests and misery and rehousing. Compulsory purchases of properties began in 1962.

Demonstrators interrupted the transport minister, Michael Heseltine, as he tried to cut the ribbon. People left living in roads beside the flyover and its years of construction unfurled a roof-height banner that demanded: 'Get us out of this hell – re-house us now.' One resident remembered: 'There was a terrible noise for weeks when they were pile-driving. They started at six o'clock in the morning. Sometimes it went on all night. You think the whole city is being bombarded beneath you.'

Michael Heseltine admitted: 'There are two sides to this business. One is the exciting road building side but there is also the human side of this thing, and how huge roads like this affect people living alongside them. You cannot but have sympathy for these people.'

Westway was anything but an ordinary road. It was at the time the longest elevated road in Europe. It was also a formal motorway, the A40(M), the first in inner London. It was the wonder of the age so far as planners were concerned, but in 2000 it was demoted to just another urban road. It is one of the few remnants of an ambitious and destructive scheme to build fast, inner ring roads within the capital.

The London Ringways project was outlined during post-war planning in 1943 and adopted by the Greater London Council a decade and a half later. Westway was its first realisation, designed with three lanes in each direction. It ran above ground because that was cheaper and needed less land. The elevated part of the M4 motorway out of London had encouraged that belief.

It did, though, mean buying slums between Harrow Road and the Grand Union Canal, which the GLC had already done, and demolishing 600 buildings and uprooting or closing off roads that had been neighbourhoods and routes to friends, shops and work for those who lived there. Some parts of the elevated road were planned to pass within 20ft of homes. There were none of the studies of environmental impact that exist today. Nor was there an obligation to compensate anyone not next to the road but nevertheless affected by the noise of its construction and use.

There were repeated protests that the road was built not where the rich lived but in poor neighbourhoods of people unable to hire lawyers and architects. The cost and public opposition meant the London Ringways were cancelled in 1973. Government proposals in 2013 to build a separated cycle path along Westway were abandoned in 2016.

It would have slowed the traffic.

1978

A ROBBER'S LAST STAND

Lean men with hollow cheeks, glasses and the air of broken dreams are not uncommon in the Edgware Road. Parts of it are prosperous, most of it is not. When you run out of money, it's the kind of place to find a small, cheap flat.

Few people knew that the old man who shuffled down the street each day had once had part of a £2,631,684 fortune – about £40 million today. Now he was penniless. What was left of the £150,000 he had pocketed let him buy a cup of tea and a bacon sandwich but little more. Riches to rags, indeed.

The man's name was Bruce Reynolds. Before dawn on 8 August 1963, he led a gang of fifteen that covered a railway signal in rural Buckinghamshire and brought the Glasgow–London night express to an unexpected halt. The gang had parked below Bridego bridge, pronounced Briddy-go, off the road between Ivinghoe at the foot of the Chilterns and the twin towns of Leighton Buzzard and Linslade, where the robbers were first tried. Police told Fleet Street reporters sent to the scene that nothing remarkable had happened. The reporters settled into the pub that stood opposite the youth hostel in Ivinghoe and drank until their deadlines forced them to send a story.

Unknown to them, Frank Hughes, a local editor on his way home from his printers in Luton, had seen the massed police cars and refused to leave until he knew more. He then phoned hourly stories to the evening papers in London, racking up a small sum in freelance payments, while their editors and those of morning papers banged the table in frustration in this era before mobile phones.

The robbers scooped up all the used banknotes on the train and drove west to Leatherslade Farm, near the village of Brill. The police didn't know they were there or who they were but the list of crooks with the talent to pull off such a job was short. And it included Buster Reynolds. But guessing is one thing, knowing is another. In the end, the robbers who had planned everything so well were uncovered by a boy collecting the numbers of passing cars. That was a hobby at the time.

The police looked at his collection and saw that just one wasn't registered locally. It had a London registration. The driver hadn't changed the number and now detectives had their first clue. More than that, a farmworker had grown suspicious of the amount of traffic at Leatherslade and suggested the police take a look. The robbers got wind of it and fled, leaving the farm without clearing it up.

The police found twenty empty mailbags, a 3ft hole and a shovel. Shelves in the house held food for a long stay. The raid's vehicles were hidden nearby. The robbers had moved in a hurry and had wiped most surfaces free of fingerprints. But detectives found prints on a Monopoly board. Reynolds' were on a sauce bottle. A week later, the police arrested a florist, Roger Cordrey, in Bournemouth. From there they arrested his accomplices.

Reynolds and his wife used fake passports to go to Mexico. They and their young son rented a penthouse in Mexico City and travelled to Acapulco and Las Vegas. They watched nervously as the other robbers were sentenced to as much as thirty years. Reynolds and his wife were joined in exile in December 1964 by Buster Edwards, who was yet to be caught, and Charlie Wilson, who had escaped from Winson Green prison.

Reynolds knew the money couldn't last for ever. He planned to steal Canadian dollars in Montreal, but the police there got wind of it and he moved to the south of France instead, and then back to London, to a mews in Kensington. There, he and his wife bought groceries from Harrods and drank Veuve Clicquot champagne.

By now, there was little of the haul left to spend. The Flying Squad was closing in and Reynolds moved to Torquay in Devon. And there, in the villa he and his wife rented, Tommy Butler arrested him in November 1968 after chasing him for years. Reynolds shrugged: '*C'est la vie*,' he said in his marked South London accent.

He pleaded guilty at Buckinghamshire assizes and was jailed for twenty-five years. He left on parole in 1978 but by then the world had changed. He struggled to cope. He was named in a small amphetamine conspiracy, which he denied, and went back to prison for three years.

He came out, alone and penniless, this once dapper man in made-to-measure suits who had lived in a Mexican penthouse, and he lived in a tiny flat off the Edgware Road. He shuffled unknown and probably unkempt to the shops most days, counted his money before he handed it over, then returned to his lonely anonymity. He moved from there back to south London, where he once wanted to be a racing cyclist, and died there in his sleep in the early hours of 28 February 2013.

'He was an intelligent man with a very dry humour,' an acquaintance remembered. 'He didn't smile easily. He could have been very successful had he not lived his life as a criminal and I think that's something he realised later on when it was too late.'

The most colourful of the Train Robbers was Ronnie Biggs. His role had been minor but he became a celebrity after he escaped to Rio de Janeiro and defied the police to catch him as they had caught Reynolds. Biggs returned to England in 2001 as he became old and infirm. He came out of jail to be wheeled to Highgate cemetery, where he and Reynolds were united once more in August 2013, fifty years after Bridego Bridge. The occasion was a memorial service. Biggs watched worldlessly, unable to speak because of a stroke. He died in a care home in Barnet, north London, in December 2013.

Reynolds is buried near another of the cemetery's occupants, Karl Marx. Reynolds' son, Nick, scattered some of the ashes he had saved from the funeral. The headstone names both Reynolds and his wife, Frances, known as Angela. Reynolds is shown, eyes closed, mouth downturned. The stone quotes the words 'This is it' and '*C'est la vie*', which Reynolds spoke as the handcuffs snapped into place.

1985

FOOTBALL KICKS OFF

Trouble has kicked off in football since football began. The game was born from undisciplined mob battles in the thirteenth century as rival towns or villages tried to kick a ball against the opposing side's church door. That achieved both a victory and a denigration of the losers' religious honour. Injuries were rife and some reports say players died. And nor did the life-threatening violence end when football's rules were codified and conventional games organised.

Fans fought each other when Aston Villa and Preston North End played in 1885. The *Penny Illustrated Paper* said of the game between Bolton and Glossop in 1908:

> No fewer than three players were sent off the field during the game, which was admittedly very vigorous indeed. Cuffe was the first sent off, and then a stand-up fight took place, with the result that Marsh and Hofton were ordered off. The referee was Mr. W. Gilgryst … [he] had to be escorted from the field to the dressing-room by the police and others, and was struck a severe blow from behind, the offender being taken in to custody. Furthermore, an official of the club was reported for using filthy language and for abusive conduct … I am afraid there is serious trouble.

Six thousand fans rioted in 1909 when officials refused to let a game between Glasgow and Celtic run to extra time to settle a draw. Countless fans and fifty-four policemen were injured; the ground was damaged and reports say that almost every street lamp was wrecked around the ground.

That, then, was the background to yet more violence around football since the 1960s and later, and, in particular, a mass fight that broke out in the Edgware Road on 12 October 1985. On that day, Chelsea played Everton. Everton were the better team but Chelsea were on home ground. The rivalry that was already there was exaggerated by rivalry between north and south.

Everton lost 2–1, missing a penalty and having a player sent off within five minutes. Police with dogs waited outside the ground. Those on the Everton side insist that the police referred to them as 'Scouse bastards' even though they came from all over the country. One remembered:

We were escorted to Fulham Broadway Tube station. Amazingly all the gates were open and we were herded on to waiting trains. As one was filled and left, another arrived. We arranged to get off at the first station we stopped at. Unfortunately, we didn't stop, at least not until we arrived at Edgware Road. As the train we were on pulled into Edgware Road Tube station, it was attacked by literally hundreds of Chelsea fans who proceeded to attack the train with baseball bats, bricks, metal bars and their Dr Martens [boots]. The next few minutes were mad; having attacked the train unhindered for some time, the Chelsea fans were 'dispersed' by more police than I have ever seen in one place at the same time … Once the platform was clear, we expected that we would head on our way …

Twenty minutes later, after the mayhem had subsided, myself and a friend found [a] young lad (he was 14) sitting on the exit steps with blood pouring down his face from a number of head wounds. Living in London, we knew that St Mary's hospital was opposite the station exit. We explained and asked if we could take him to A&E and were told in no uncertain terms by the police blocking the stairs that 'nobody is leaving the station.' At that point, the lad's father found us. He was an off-duty Merseyside police officer, he showed his warrant card and still they would not allow the lad treatment.

Another fan, Mick Davies, remembered:

The Chelsea fans were like savages, throwing fire extinguishers through the Tube train windows and wading in with iron bars and whatever else they could find. The train floors were covered in blood and every single window was shattered … Back at Euston, it was like the arrival of the Dunkirk evacuees arriving at Dover: everyone had horror stories and most had injuries and blood-soaked clothing. And we were the lucky ones. A few were in hospital and didn't get home for a few days.

The *Sunday Times* that year called football 'a slum sport, watched by slum people, in slum stadiums'.

The mass fights inside and outside grounds have lessened. Battered fans may no longer be left with rival fans' cards to say they have been 'visited'. But the 'slum sport, watched by slum people' is still far from peaceful. The BBC reported in January 2022:

Arrests at football matches across the top five English leagues are at their highest levels in years, with fan disorder "getting worse", according to the UK's football policing lead. The latest data covers the first half of this season – which has seen the return of fans to capacity stadiums after a year of lockdowns and restrictions. There have been more than 800 football-related arrests in the first six months of the season, alongside more than 750 reported incidents of disorder.

2014

GEORGE AND THE ROMANIANS

North London has always been a place of immigration. Most pass through unremarked, which is no more than they'd hoped. Others found fame. Or, if they didn't, their children did. Take young Kyriacos Panayiotou, for instance. He and his cousin left their village in Cyprus in 1953 and emigrated to East Finchley. Kyriacos found work as a waiter and in the evenings went dancing. Through dancing, he met and married Lesley and they had two daughters and then a son. Needing more space, they moved to Burnt Oak and a flat above shops at 3a Holmstall Parade, on the Edgware Road. There's still a Greek restaurant on the ground floor.

Kyriacos quickly found that nobody could pronounce his name; he obliged by shortening it to Jack Panos. His son, Georgios, called himself George. And then George Michael. He and his musical partner, Andrew Ridgeley, played their last date as Wham! down the road at Wembley. Michael died in 2016, aged 53.

Greek speakers such as Michael's father say *Geia sou* when they greet each other. Later immigrants say *buna* and then *ce faci?* The first – 'boona' – is a casual contraction of the phrase for 'good day'. The second is pronounced *chay futch*, and it asks how you are.

The language is Romanian, one of the Latin group that has sisters in French, Spanish, Portuguese and Italian. Linguists sometimes say that if Latin still existed, it would be Romanian. But of all the so-called romance languages (because the first popular books were written in what had become of Latin), Romanian is alone in not neighbouring another language in the family. It has gone its own sweet way, therefore, maintaining sentence constructions that are a reminder of its Latin roots, adopting words from neighbouring Slavic languages, and above all going wholesale for a process called assibilation. That's the word for what happens when languages change hard sounds for soft ones, as English has done from *kirk* to *church*. Romanian's enthusiasm for this softening gives it its ch-ch-ch sound.

There are now more Romanians in Britain than Irish and Indians. There were 163,000 in London in 2019, say government figures. That makes them the capital's largest community of foreigners. They work in many jobs but particularly in low-paid service work: stocking supermarkets, looking after the poor and ill, and cleaning your hotel room after you've left. Many of them live in Burnt Oak and Edgware.

But not everything about Romanians – some Romanians – is quite so soft as that *ch-ch-ch*. Ţăndărei is just a little north-east from the capital, Bucharest, two thirds of the way to the Black Sea and the end of Europe. A little more than 13,000 people live there.

It's hard to deny claims that it's a Beverly Hills for Romanian gangsters. Dragoş, a chef who speaks five languages, came from there to work in England. He showed photos of his town to a *Guardian* reporter. 'Every shepherd has its black sheep, so do countries,' he said. Criminals there give all Romanians a bad name, he says. He showed videos of fancy cars and lavish mansions in Ţăndărei. 'We don't have any future in Romania because of the corruption,' he said.

That corruption has spread wide. It doesn't, of course, concern more than a minority of Romanians, who are embarrassed by the reputation the community has acquired. As ever, it's the minority that attract attention and not the honest majority. Nevertheless, Romanian beggars stand in the Edgware Road at its southern end and wait in the tunnels of Underground stations. They typically hold a small child, regardless of the cold. Some are said to pester travellers at bus stops. The London police ran a joint operation with their Romanian counterparts, Operation Golf. They traced the begging to gangs in Ţăndărei.

Girls sent to England can be 16 or younger. 'It's been going on for years and it's vast in scale,' Inspector Michael Wright told reporters. 'It's specifically females from Romania. They have learnt over the years and changed their costumes. Nowadays they wear headscarves and make themselves look more Arabic so that it is harder for the Arabic community to see that they are, in fact, Romanian. The problem of begging is likely to continue.'

Nobody knows for certain how much beggars raise. It's not a business accustomed to accountancy. But the belief is that the girls are installed in cheap flats in Slough and the Essex suburbs and then commute to London in general and the Edgware Road in particular. The money goes back to Ţăndărei and explains the villas and expensive cars in one of the poorest countries in Europe.

Now that the police accept that they can't stop it, they have switched to telling the Middle Eastern community in English and Arabic that the girls aren't Arab despite their head scarves and that they are unlikely to be Muslim. The Koran urges Muslims to be charitable, not to be swindled.

But why so far out on the Northern Line? Why Burnt Oak?

Marius Pepoo Marius told a reporter from *My London* that he came in 2007 and chose Burnt Oak because so many Romanians went there before him. That doesn't explain why the first Romanians came, of course, but it does explain Marius's arrival.

And what in particular persuaded him? The food.

He said:

> It was hard to find Romanian food before 2014 in London as there weren't
> many places. When I came here to Burnt Oak, I was blown away. There were
> so many restaurants. It was like having my mum's cooking but without having
> my mum – if that makes any sense. So it was really exciting for me. I was trying
> all the different foods that I couldn't get from the shops. They make really nice
> food here and it's not expensive.

The best restaurant in Burnt Oak, he said, was the Brasseria Timisoreana. And that's
significant because it was in Timisoara that the revolution began that overthrew
Nicolae Ceauşescu. Of all the communist leaders in Europe, he alone was overthrown
by street protest. Romania swims fish-shape into Europe, which is symbolic in its way.

But, like all immigrants, Romanians are not always welcomed. Kroky is a fast-
food shop that displays its name over the blue, yellow and red of the national flag. Its
owner, Andrei Liviu Chiroşcă, received an unsigned letter:

> You should have gone back to Rumania [*sic*], with your gypsies. You are not
> welcome here – And never will be. We hope the Brexit will stop any more
> from coming Here. We are sick of not hearing our own language in our own
> country. We never go to Watling Avenue shopping centre, 12 greengrocers,
> the rest are cheap clothes shops and tatty gift shops (none of these shops are
> English). So, there is no point in going to this shopping centre. You will only
> get Romanians in your shop and hopefully you will not last long and we can
> see the back of you.

Burnt Oak is commonly pronounced *bontoc*. Ovidiu Sarpe runs a restaurant there.
She told reporters: 'When I arrived as a refugee in 1979, everybody wanted to know
about Romania and what it was like to live under communism. I was proud of my
identity. Now I avoid speaking Romanian in the street. But I never had any problem
in this country, and now we are no longer immigrants, we are European citizens. It's
the times and, you know, the masses – you need to give them a little circus.'

THE END OF THE ROAD

And the Edgware Road after Edgware? It carries on north for a short distance. It skirts the edge of Metroland as it passes Stanmore. And …

Metroland? Well, just as Burnt Oak grew with the Northern Line station, so a whole swathe of suburbs – Wembley, Harrow, Pinner, Harrow Weald and Ruislip, among others – appeared in formerly empty fields because of the Metropolitan Railway. The Metropolitan was the one part of the Underground that had true ambitions to become a main-line service. It ran steam trains in shallow tunnels and through underground stations it hoped were wide enough to lessen the smoke it inflicted on customers. It was planned at its peak to run for 80km, even further into the countryside of Buckinghamshire than it does now.

The directors' ambitions were not to make transport easier for those in cut-off villages. They were far more cynical. They set out to create suburbs, leafy paradises of wide streets and spacious houses, and thereby create commuters for their trains. In an era with neither planning rules nor a Green Belt – the ring of supposed rurality intended to halt London's spread – the company set up a Metropolitan Surplus Lands Committee.

That was 1887. Three years later, it built its first housing estate at Pinner, west from Stanmore on the road to Rickmansworth. It carried on from there and, knowing few people would know where to find what had until then been only villages, it coined the name Metroland in 1915 to promote a cohesive whole.

One history says:

The default architectural style of these new leafy suburbs was Tudorbethan, a mix of traditional styles on the exterior, matched by the comforts of modernity inside. Modernism was the upcoming style of the era, spreading to Britain from Europe, and examples can be found throughout Metroland.

London Transport's own assessment is that, 'The reality of row upon row of suburban houses may have differed from the publicists' image of semi-rural tranquillity, but Metro-land did offer more space, access to the countryside and a better quality of life for the people who moved out of London's cramped inner-city areas.'

Edgware was saved Metroland's spread and countryside begins just beyond the junction to Stanmore as the Edgware Road begins its climb of Brockley Hill. At the top is the Royal National Orthopaedic Hospital, created in 1922 from a merger of the Royal Orthopaedic and City Orthopaedic hospitals. Further down Wood Lane to the left is Pear Wood Scout camp and then the Shree Swaminarayan temple.

The main road then drops to the junction with the M1 and the Edgware Way bypass, by now the road to the Buckinghamshire county town of Aylesbury. Just beyond the junction, on the Aylesbury road, are the remains of supports on which the Northern Line was to have continued to Bushey Heath on the edge of Watford.

The road climbs again, heading north-east now rather than north-west, to Elstree – and confusion. Confusion one is the name. A topographer, Daniel Lyson, said at the end of the 1700s that:

The name of this place has been variously written Eaglestree, Elstree, Ilstrye, Idlestrye, etc. Norden says that it is called, in Offa's grant to the Abbey of St Alban's, Eaglestree, that is, says he, *Nemus aquilinum*, a 'place where it may be thought that eagles bred in time past.' It has been derived also from Idel-street, i.e. the noble road; and Ill-street, the decayed road. May it not have been, rather, a corruption of Eald-street, the old road, i.e. the ancient Watling-street, upon which it is situated?

Which may not be entirely clear.

Confusion two is that the film and now television studios by which many know Elstree aren't in Elstree at all, but are some distance away in the newer town of Borehamwood. The studios preceded the town. The first to be built there was in 1914. Borehamwood, as an expansion town for Londoners, followed decades later, after the war. But the studios do not lie on the Edgware Road and so, sadly, their rich history isn't part of the our history.

That history, in just 10 miles, spans not just centuries, as do all roads, but a history surely unrivalled anywhere else.

It's been a wonderful journey. I hope you enjoyed it as much as I did.